Amelia

Poems

Thirteenth Edition

Amelia

Poems
Thirteenth Edition

ISBN/EAN: 9783744704373

Printed in Europe, USA, Canada, Australia, Japan

Cover: Foto ©Thomas Meinert / pixelio.de

More available books at **www.hansebooks.com**

POEMS.

BY

AMELIA.

THIRTEENTH EDITION, ENLARGED.

THIRTEENTH THOUSAND.

NEW-YORK:
D. APPLETON & CO., 346 & 348 BROADWAY.
M.DCCC.LVI.

TO

MY BELOVED FATHER

THIS VOLUME IS DEDICATED,

AS A SLIGHT TRIBUTE OF LOVE

BY HIS

AFFECTIONATE DAUGHTER

AMELIA.

CONTENTS.

	PAGE
THE RAINBOW,	9
I WEEP NOT,	12
THE SUMMER BIRDS,	16
I HAVE A FAIR AND GENTLE FRIEND,	20
O! DARK IS THE GLOOM,	24
THE GREEN MOSSY BANK,	26
MUSINGS,	28
TO THE SKY-LARK,	33
TO A LOVELY GIRL,	38
LINES TO A LADY,	40
MELODIA,	44
LINES WRITTEN ON A MINIATURE,	48
I KNOW THAT THY SPIRIT,	51
WHEN SHINES THE STAR,	54
MY SISTERS,	58
THE FIRST DEATH OF THE HOUSEHOLD,	62
THE MAIDEN'S FIRST LOVE,	66
THE STARS,	69
STANZAS,	74
TIME,	79
THE FREED BIRD,	82
THE CAPTIVE SAILOR-BOY,	86
THE GOLDEN RINGLET,	90
THE COTTAGE BAND,	94
THE LITTLE STEP-SON,	97
TO A HUMMING-BIRD,	99
THE BROKEN-HEARTED,	102
THE YOUNG LOVERS,	105
THE BLIND GIRL'S LAMENT,	108
TO ——,	112
HE CAME TOO LATE,	115
THE AMERICAN SWORD,	119
VIOLA,	122

CONTENTS.

	PAGE
To the Evening Star,	124
Breathe not a sigh,	127
The Dying Girl,	130
The Neglected Harp,	136
The Stars,	139
The Dew-Drop,	142
The Sleeping Maiden,	144
My own Native Land,	147
To Mrs. S. J. P——,	149
The Dying Mother,	151
Sweet be thy dreams,	156
The Violet's Song to the Lost Fairy,	158
The Sea-Shell,	161
To Mrs. L——,	165
Lines on seeing a beautiful little Girl gathering Flowers,	167
The Dreamers,	171
May,	175
Pulpit Eloquence,	179
The Last Interview,	185
When soft stars,	189
O! had we only met,	191
To Amanda,	194
Music,	196
The Bride,	199
The Mournful Heart,	203
The Parted Year,	206
I never have loved thee,	212
On seeing an Infant sleeping on its Mother's Bosom,	215
The Presence of God,	217
I know thee not,	222
Thou canst not forget me,	225
Hopeless Love,	228
The Bereaved,	232
To Lucy during her Absence,	235
On entering the Mammoth Cave,	237
Sudden Death,	245
I saw thee but a moment,	249
The Evening Skies,	252
The Old Maid,	255
The Brother's Lament	259
One word with thee,	263

POEMS.

THE RAINBOW.

I SOMETIMES have thoughts, in my loneliest hours,
That lie on my heart like the dew on the flowers,
Of a ramble I took one bright afternoon
When my heart was as light as a blossom in June;
The green earth was moist with the late fallen showers,
The breeze fluttered down and blew open the flowers,
While a single white cloud, to its haven of rest
On the white wing of peace, floated off in the west.

As I threw back my tresses to catch the cool breeze,
That scattered the rain-drops and dimpled the seas,
Far up the blue sky a fair rainbow unrolled
Its soft-tinted pinions of purple and gold.

'Twas born in a moment, yet, quick as its birth,
It had stretched to the uttermost ends of the earth,
And, fair as an angel, it floated as free,
With a wing on the earth and a wing on the sea.

How calm was the ocean! how gentle its swell!
Like a woman's soft bosom it rose and it fell;
While its light sparkling waves, stealing laughingly o'er,
When they saw the fair rainbow, knelt down on the shore.
No sweet hymn ascended, no murmur of prayer,
Yet I felt that the spirit of worship was there,
And bent my young head, in devotion and love,
'Neath the form of the angel, that floated above.

How wide was the sweep of its beautiful wings!
How boundless its circle! how radiant its rings!
If I looked on the sky, 'twas suspended in air;
If I looked on the ocean, the rainbow was there;
Thus forming a girdle, as brilliant and whole
As the thoughts of the rainbow, that circled my soul.
Like the wing of the Deity, calmly unfurled,
It bent from the cloud and encircled the world.

There are moments, I think, when the spirit receives
Whole volumes of thought on its unwritten leaves,
When the folds of the heart in a moment unclose
Like the innermost leaves from the heart of a rose.
And thus, when the rainbow had passed from the sky,
The thoughts it awoke were too deep to pass by;
It left my full soul, like the wing of a dove,
All fluttering with pleasure, and fluttering with love.

I know that each moment of rapture or pain
But shortens the links in life's mystical chain;
I know that my form, like that bow from the wave,
Must pass from the earth, and lie cold in the grave;
Yet O! when death's shadows my bosom encloud,
When I shrink at the thought of the coffin and shroud,
May Hope, like the rainbow, my spirit enfold
In her beautiful pinions of purple and gold.

"I WEEP NOT."

I weep not as I wept
    When first they laid thee low;
My sorrow all too deep is kept
    To melt like common wo;
    Nor do my lips e'er part
    With whispers of thy name,
But thou art shrined in this hushed heart,
    And that is all the same.

    I could be happy now,
    Had memory flown with thee,
But I still hear a whisper low,
    And memory will not flee;

A whisper that doth tell
Of thee, and thee alone,
A memory, like the ocean-shell,
Forever making moan.

For how can I forget
Thine eye of softest brown,
With its pale lid, just touched with jet,
And always drooping down;
And thy sweet form of grace,
That went to rest too soon,
And the turning up of thy young face
Beneath the placid moon!

I sometimes think thy hand
Is on my forehead pressed,
And almost feel thy tresses, fanned
Across my beating breast,
And catch the sunny flow
Of thy mantle on the air,
And turn to see if it is so—
Alas! thou art not there!

And I wander out alone
 Beside the singing rills,
When nothing but the wind's low tone
 Comes stealing down the hills;
 And while along the deep
 The moonbeams softly shine,
My silent soul goes forth to keep
 Its blessed tryste with thine.

 I weep not though thou'rt laid
 In such a lone dark place,
Thou, who didst live without a snade,
 To cloud thy sweet young face;
 For now thy spirit sings
 Where angel-ones have trod,
Veiling their faces 'neath their wings
 Around the throne of God.

 Thy faults were slight and few
 As human faults could be,
And thy virtues were as many too
 As gems beneath the sea;

And thy thoughts did heavenward roam
    Until, like links of gold,
They drew thee up to thy blue home
    Within the Saviour's fold.

THE SUMMER BIRDS.

Sweet warblers of the sunny hours,
    Forever on the wing—
I love them as I love the flowers,
    The sunlight and the spring.
They come like pleasant memories
    In summer's joyous time,
And sing their gushing melodies
    As I would sing a rhyme.

In the green and quiet places,
    Where the golden sunlight falls,
We sit with smiling faces
    To list their silver calls.

And when their holy anthems
    Come pealing through the air,
Our hearts leap forth to meet them
    With a blessing and a prayer.

Amid the morning's fragrant dew,
    Amid the mists of even,
They warble on as if they drew
    Their music down from heaven.
How sweetly sounds each mellow note
    Beneath the moon's pale ray,
When dying zephyrs rise and float
    Like lovers' sighs away!

Like shadowy spirits seen at eve,
    Among the tombs they glide,
Where sweet pale forms, for which we grieve,
    Lie sleeping side by side.
They break with song the solemn hush
    Where peace reclines her head,
And link their lays with mournful thoughts,
    That cluster round the dead.

For never can my soul forget
    The loved of other years;
Their memories fill my spirit yet—
    I've kept them green with tears;
And their singing greets my heart at times
    As in the days of yore,
Though their music and their loveliness
    Is ever o'er—forever o'er.

And often, when the mournful night
    Comes with a low sweet tune,
And sets a star on every height
    And one beside the moon,
When not a sound of wind or wave
    The holy stillness mars,
I look above and strive to trace
    Their dwellings in the stars.

The birds of summer hours—
    They bring a gush of glee
To the child among the dewy flowers,
    To the sailor on the sea.

THE SUMMER BIRDS.

We hear their thrilling voices
  In their swift and airy flight,
And the inmost heart rejoices
  With a calm and pure delight.

In the stillness of the starlight hours,
  When I am with the dead,
O! may they flutter mid the flowers,
  That blossom o'er my head,
And pour their songs of gladness forth
  In one melodious strain,
O'er lips, whose broken melody
  Shall never sing again.

I HAVE A FAIR AND GENTLE FRIEND.

I have a fair and gentle friend,
   Whose heart is pure, I ween,
As ever was a maiden's heart
   At joyous seventeen;
She dwells among us like a star,
   That, from its bower of bliss,
Looks down, yet gathers not a stain
   From aught it sees in this.

I do not mean that flattery
   Has never reached her ear;
I only say its syren song
   Has no effect on her;

For she is all simplicity,
    A creature soft and mild—
Though on the eve of womanhood,
    In heart a very child.

And yet, within the misty depths
    Of her dark dreamy eyes,
A shadowy something, like deep thought,
    In tender sadness lies;
For though her glance still shines as bright
    As in her childish years,
Its wildness and its lustre, now,
    Are softened down by tears:—

Tears, that steal not from hidden springs
    Of sorrow and regret,
For none but lovely feelings
    In her gentle breast have met,
For every tear that gems her eye,
    From her young bosom flows
Like dew-drops from a golden star,
    Or perfume from a rose.

HAVE A FAIR AND GENTLE FRIEND.

For e'en in life's delicious spring,
   We oft have memories
That throw around our sunny hearts
   A transient cloud of sighs;
For a wondrous change within the heart
   At that sweet time is wrought,
When on the heart is softly laid
   A spell of deeper thought.

And she has reached that lovely time,
   That sweet poetic age,
When to the eye each floweret's leaf
   Seems like a glowing page;
For a beauty and a mystery
   About the heart are thrown,
When childhood's merry laughter yields
   To girlhood's softer tone.

I do not know if round her heart
   Love yet hath thrown his wing,
I rather think she's like myself
   An April-hearted thing;

I HAVE A FAIR AND GENTLE FRIEND.

I only know that she is fair,
And loves me passing well;
But who this gentle maiden is
I feel not free to tell.

O! DARK IS THE GLOOM.

O! DARK is the gloom o'er my young spirit stealing!
　Then why should I linger where others are gay!
The smile that I wear, is but worn for concealing
　A heart that is wasting in sadness away!

How oft have I thought, when the last light has faded
　From off the clear waves of some soft-flowing stream,
That, like its bright waters, my last hopes were shaded
　By darkness, uncheered by the light of a beam.

O! could I but fly from this false world forever,
　Where those whom I trust are the first to betray,
From the cold and the fickle my young heart I'd sever
　Ere they steal all its bloom and its sweetness away.

I'd seek, in some orb of the blessed above me,
　The peace that on earth I can never receive;
The spirits that dwell in that bright orb would love me,
　For they are too gentle to wound or deceive.

O! why should the hearts of the purest be shaken,
　While calmly reposing 'neath love's sunny beam?
If they slumber so sweetly, why should they awaken
　To muse on the past, and to weep o'er a dream?

THE GREEN MOSSY BANK WHERE THE BUTTER-CUPS GREW.

O MY thoughts are away where my infancy flew,
Near the green mossy bank where the buttercups grew,
Where the bright silver fountain eternally played,
First laughing in sunshine, then singing in shade;
There oft in my childhood I've wandered in play,
Flinging up the cool drops of the light falling spray,
Till my small naked feet were all bathed in bright dew,
As I played on the bank where the buttercups grew.

How softly that green bank sloped down from the hill
To the spot where the fountain grew suddenly still!
How cool was the shadow the long branches gave,
As they hung from the willow and dipped in the wave!

And then, each pale lily, that slept on the stream,
Rose and fell with the wave, as if stirred by a dream!
While my home 'mid the vine-leaves rose soft on my view,
As I played on the bank where the buttercups grew.

The beautiful things! how I watched them unfold,
Till they lifted their delicate vases of gold!
O, never a spot since those days have I seen
With leaves of such freshness and flowers of such sheen!
How glad was my spirit! for then there was naught
To burden its wing, save some beautiful thought
Breaking up from its depths with each wild wind that blew
O'er the green mossy bank where the buttercups grew.

The paths I have trod I would quickly retrace,
Could I win back the gladness, that looked from my face
As I cooled my warm lip in that fountain, I love
With a spirit as pure as the wing of a dove—
Could I wander again where my forehead was starred
With the beauty that dwelt in my bosom unmarred,
And, calm as a child in the starlight and dew,
Fall asleep on the bank where the buttercups grew.

MUSINGS.

I wandered out one summer-night,
   'Twas when my years were few
The wind was singing in the light.
   And I was singing too:
The sunshine lay upon the hill,
   The shadow in the vale,
And here and there a leaping rill
   Was laughing on the gale.

One fleecy cloud upon the air
   Was all that met my eyes;
It floated like an angel there
   Between me and the skies;

I clapped my hands and warbled wild,
  As here and there I flew,
For I was but a careless child
  And did as children do.

The waves came dancing o'er the sea
  In bright and glittering bands;
Like little children, wild with glee,
  They linked their dimpled hands—
They linked their hands, but, ere I caught
  Their sprinkled drops of dew,
They kissed my feet, and, quick as thought,
  Away the ripples flew.

The twilight hours, like birds, flew by,
  As lightly and as free;
Ten thousand stars were in the sky,
  Ten thousand on the sea;
For every wave with dimpled face,
  That leaped upon the air,
Had caught a star in its embrace,
  And held it trembling there.

MUSINGS.

The young moon too with upturned sides
   Her mirrored beauty gave,
And, as a bark at anchor rides,
   She rode upon the wave;
The sea was like the heaven above,
   As perfect and as whole,
Save that it seemed to thrill with love
   As thrills the immortal soul.

The leaves, by spirit-voices stirred,
   Made murmurs on the air,
Low murmurs, that my spirit heard
   And answered with a prayer;
For 'twas upon that dewy sod,
   Beside the moaning seas,
I learned at first to worship God
   And sing such strains as these.

The flowers, all folded to their dreams,
   Were bowed in slumber free
By breezy hills and murmuring streams,
   Where'er they chanced to be;

No guilty tears had they to weep,
    No sins to be forgiven ;
They closed their leaves and went to sleep
    'Neath the blue eye of heaven.

No costly robes upon them shone,
    No jewels from the seas,
Yet Solomon, upon his throne,
    Was ne'er arrayed like these ;
And just as free from guilt and art
    Were lovely human flowers,
Ere sorrow set her bleeding heart
    On this fair world of ours.

I heard the laughing wind behind
    A-playing with my hair ;
The breezy fingers of the wind—
    How cool and moist they were !
I heard the night-bird warbling o'er
    Its soft enchanting strain ;
I never heard such sounds before,
    And never shall again.

Then wherefore weave such strains as these
    And sing them day by day,
When every bird upon the breeze
    Can sing a sweeter lay!
I'd give the world for their sweet art,
    The simple, the divine—
I'd give the world to melt one heart
    As they have melted mine.

TO THE SKY-LARK.

Thou little bird, thou lov'st to dwell
   Beneath the summer leaves!
The sunlight round thy mossy cell
   A golden halo weaves;
And the sweet dews, where'er we pass,
Like living diamonds gem the grass,
   And round the mossy eaves
The twittering swallow circling flies,
As happy as the laughing skies.

Soft as a bride, the rosy dawn
   From dewy sleep doth rise,
And, bathed in blushes, hath withdrawn
   The mantle from her eyes;

TO THE SKY-LARK.

And, with her orbs dissolved in dew,
Bends like an angel softly through
  The blue-pavilioned skies.
Then up, and pour thy mellow lay,
To greet the young and radiant day!

Hark! now with low and fluttering start,
  The sky-lark soars above,
And from her full melodious heart
  She pours her strains of love;
And now her quivering wings fling back
The golden light that floods her track,
  Now scarcely seems to move,
But floats awhile on waveless wings,
Then soars away, and, soaring, sings.

Bird of the pure and dewy morn!
  How soft thy heavenward lay
Floats up, where light and life are born
  Around the rosy day!

And, as the balm that fills the hour
Lies soft upon each waving flower,
  The happy wind at play
Tells, as its voice goes laughing by,
The lark is singing in the sky.

When shall thy fearless wing find rest,
  Bird of the dewy hours?
When wilt thou seek thy little nest,
  Close hid among the flowers?
Not till the bright clouds, one by one,
Are marshalled round the setting sun,
  In heaven's celestial bowers,
Shall the old forest round thee fling
Its mournful shades, O lonely thing!

Lonely! and did I call thee lone?
  'Twas but a careless word:
The round blue heaven is all thine own,
  O free and happy bird!

TO THE SKY-LARK.

Wherever laughs a singing rill,
Or points to heaven a verdant hill,
   Thy waving wing hath stirred;
For all sweet things, where'er they be,
Are like familiar friends to thee.

Could I, O living lute of heaven!
   But learn to act thy part,
And use the gift so freely given,
   That floods my inmost heart;
Each morn, my melting strains of love
Should rise like thine to Him above,
   Who made thee what thou art,
And spread abroad each waving tree,
For thee, O little bird! for thee.

And shall the poet envy thee,
   Bird of the quivering wing,
Whose soul immortal, swift, and free,
   Should ever soar and sing?

TO THE SKY-LARK.

Predestined for a loftier flight,
The spirit, filled with heavenly light,
  From this cold earth shall spring,
And soar where thou canst never roam,
Bird of the blue and breezy dome

O! if our hearts were never stirred.
  By harsher sounds than these—
The low sweet singing of a bird,
  The murmur of the breeze,—
How soft would glide our fleeting hours
Blessed as the sunshine and the flowers,
  And calm as summer seas!
Linked hand in hand with Love and Hope
We'd wander down life's flowery slope.

TO A LOVELY GIRL.

Thou art not beautiful, yet thy young face
Makes up in sweetness, what it lacks in grace;
Thou art not beautiful, yet thy blue eyes
Steal o'er the heart like sunshine o'er the skies;
Theirs is the mild and intellectual ray,
That to the inmost spirit wins its way;
Theirs are the beams, that full upon you roll,
Surprising all the senses and the soul;
For O, when, pure as heaven's serenest skies,
Thy timid soul sits pleading in thine eyes,
The humid beams that 'neath thine eyelids steal
Can softly teach the coldest heart to feel;
For Heaven, that gives to thee each mental grace,
Hath stamped the angel on thy sweet young face.
O! while the pearl of peace securely dwells
Deep in thy tender heart's ambrosial cells,

TO A LOVELY GIRL.

While virtue sheds around thy virgin name
A light more lovely than the light of fame,
Thy sweet simplicity, thy graceful ease,
Shall please even more than beauty e'er can please;
Thy heart of softness and thy soul refined
Shall charm and win the most fastidious mind:
And, as for me, where'er my footsteps wend,
My heart brim full of thee, my happy friend!
Shall pine, when musing on thy sweet young face,
Thine airy footstep, and thy breezy grace,
To lay a soft hand 'mid thy trembling curls
And bless thee as the loveliest of girls.

LINES—TO A LADY.

LADY! my mountain-pathway wends
  Where thou wilt never dwell;
And now to thee, and all my friends,
  I wave a last farewell!
Far in the dim and distant West
  On fair Kentucky's shore,
Still dwell the friends who love me best,
  And one, whom I adore;
And there, where fairy footsteps rove,
  Entombed among the flowers
Still sleeps the friend I used to love
  In my young happy hours.

LINES—TO A LADY.

Ask you if she was young and fair?
    Her charms can ne'er be told;
The trembling lustre of her hair
    Was radiant, radiant gold.
Her mouth was like a rose-bud, wet
    In summer's softest showers;
Her eyes among the stars seemed set,
    Her feet among the flowers;
Her voice was like the softest flow
    Of some melodious breeze;
Yes, she was young and fair, but O!
    Her charms were more than these.

O, how I loved her! yet, methinks,
    Should friendship's glittering chain
Unite in bliss its broken links,
    Around my heart again,
Those soft and melting orbs of thine,
    That sparkle as they burn,
From this too tender heart of mine
    Would meet a soft return;

LINES—TO A LADY.

For, lady! till that first sweet even,
    You stole within my view,
My melting heart to her had given
    The softest throbs it drew.

O, could thy glowing fancy trace
    The form, my fancy sees—
The ringlets lifted from her face
    By every passing breeze;
The clearness of her ample brow,
    Her orbs of hazel hue
Soft melting on thee—even thou
    Wouldst love and mourn her too!
She lived as lives a peaceful dove;
    She died as blossoms die;
And now her spirit floats above,
    A seraph in the sky.

Farewell! I ask no vow of thine,
    I feel no foolish fears;
For if thy heart be formed, like mine,
    For softness and for tears,

Each whisper of the twilight breeze,
　　Each murmur of the sea,
Will fill thy heart with thoughts like these—
　　Will fill it full of me;
Each floating cloud, each trembling star,
　　Will tell a tale of one,
Who dwells from thee and thine afar,
　　Beneath the setting sun.

MELODIA.

I MET, once in my girlish hours,
  A creature, soft and warm;
Her cottage bonnet, filled with flowers,
  Hung swinging on her arm;
Her voice was sweet as the voice of Love,
  And her teeth were pure as pearls,
While her forehead lay, like a snow-white **dove,**
  In a nest of nut-brown curls;
She was a thing unknown to fame—
Melodia was her strange sweet name.

I never saw an eye so bright
  And yet so soft as hers;
It sometimes swam in liquid light,
  And sometimes swam in tears;

It seemed a beauty, set apart
    For softness and for sighs;
But O! Melodia's melting heart
    Was softer than her eyes—
For they were only formed to spread
The softness, from her spirit shed.

I've gazed on many a brighter face,
    But ne'er on one for years,
Where beauty left so soft a trace
    As it had left on hers.
But who can paint the spell, that wove
    A brightness round the whole?
'Twould take an angel from above
    To paint the immortal soul—
To trace the light, the inborn grace,
The spirit, sparkling o'er her face.

Her bosom was a soft retreat
    For love, and love alone,
And yet her heart had never beat
    To Love's delicious tone.

MELODIA.

It dwelt within its circle free
   From tender thoughts like these,
Waiting the little deity,
   As the blossom waits the breeze
Before it throws the leaves apart
And trembles, like the love-touched heart.

She was a creature, strange as fair,
   First mournful and then wild—
Now laughing on the clear bright air
   As merry as a child,
Then, melting down, as soft as even
   Beneath some new control,
She'd throw her hazel eyes to heaven
   And sing with all her soul,
In tones as rich as some young bird's,
Warbling her own delightful words.

Melodia! O how soft thy darts,
   How tender and how sweet!
Thy song enchained a thousand hearts
   And drew them to thy feet;

And, as thy bright lips sang, they caught
  So beautiful a ray,
That, as I gazed, I almost thought
  The spirit of thy lay
Had left, while melting on the air,
Its sweet expression painted there.

Sweet vision of that starry even!
  Thy virgin beauty yet,
Next to the blessed hope of heaven,
  Is in my spirit set.
It is a something, shrined apart,
  A light from memory, shed,
To live until this tender heart,
  On which it lives, is dead—
Reminding me of brighter hours,
Of summer eves and summer flowers.

LINES WRITTEN ON A MINIATURE.

This is the pictured likeness of my love!
How true to life! it seems to breathe and move!
Fire, love, and sweetness o'er each feature melt,
The face expressing all the spirit felt!
Here, while I gaze within those large dark eyes,
I almost see the living spirit rise;
While lights and shadows, all harmonious, glow,
And heavenly radiance settles on the brow.
And then, that mouth! how tranquil its repose!
Sleeping in fragrance like a slumbering rose,
It seems the ruby gate of love and bliss,
Just formed to murmur sighs, to smile, and kiss.
To what a lofty height can art arrive!
This glorious face, though lifeless, seems alive;

ON A MINIATURE.

The lifted lash, the shining chestnut hair,
Like nature, trembling on the ambient air.
When o'er his task the painter sat apart,
On this loved face exhausting all his art,
What were his thoughts, when, in the magic strife,
He saw each feature struggling into life,
When every kindling glance, and manly grace,
Caught from the moving form, and breathing face,
Beneath his touch, like soft enchantment stole,
And on the ivory smiled the living soul!
Flushed with delight, in that triumphant hour,
His heart expanded like an opening flower;
His hopes on airy wings were lightly raised,
And all his soul exulted as he gazed.
But ah! such thrilling joys are known to few.
They are the painter's meed, the poet's due.
And O! how sweet the bliss such joys impart,
Although their very raptures break the heart!
What, though the poet, bending o'er his lyre,
Like his own songs, in sweetness may expire!
Who would not, swan-like, waste his sweetest breath,
To taste such rapture—die so sweet a death?

ON A MINIATURE.

Flushed, faint, and trembling at his own success,
Such joys as these, the lonely painter bless.
As some fair face his silent toil repays,
And bursts in beauty on his raptured gaze,
His thoughts, too sweet for mortal hearts to share
Float up to heaven, and find an echo there,
While on his heart descends immortal fire,
And his own soul becomes his funeral pyre.

"I KNOW THAT THY SPIRIT."

I know that thy spirit looks radiantly down,
   From yon beautiful orb of the blessed,
For a sound and a sign have been set in my own,
   That tell of the place of thy rest;
For I gaze on the star that we talked of so oft,
   As our glances would heavenward rove,
When thy step was on earth, and thy bosom was soft
   With a sense of delight and of love.

The dreams, that were laid on thy shadowless brow,
   Were pure as a feeling unborn,
And the tone of thy voice was as pleasant and low
   As a bird's in a pleasant spring morn;

"I KNOW THAT THY SPIRIT."

Such a heaven of purity dwelt in thy breast,
    Such a world of bright thoughts in thy soul,
That naught could have made thee more lovely or blessed
    So bright was the beautiful whole.

But now o'er thy breast in the hush of the tomb
    Are folded thy pale graceful arms,
While the midnight of death, like a garment of gloom,
    Hangs over that bosom's young charms!
And pale, pale, alas! is thy rosy lip now,
    Its melody broken and gone,
And cold is the young heart, whose sweet dreams below
    Were of summer, of summer alone.

Yet the rise and the fall of thine eyelids of snow
    O'er their blue orbs so mournfully meek,
And the delicate blush that would vanish and glow
    Through the light of thy transparent cheek,
And thy tresses all put from thy forehead away—
    These, these on my memory rise,
As I gaze on yon bright orb, whose beautiful ray
    Hath so often been blessed by thine eyes.

"I KNOW THAT THY SPIRIT."

The blue-girdled stars and the soft dreamy air,
 Divide thy fair spirit and mine,
Yet I look in my heart, and a something is there,
 That links it in feeling to thine :
The glow of the sunset, the voice of the breeze,
 As it cradles itself on the sea,
Are dear to my bosom, for moments like these
 Are sacred to memory and thee.

"WHEN SHINES THE STAR."

When shines the star by thee loved best,
   Upon those soft delicious eves,
Lighting the ring-dove to her nest
   Where tremblings stir the darkling leaves;
When flings the wave its crest of foam
   Above the shadowy-mantled seas,
A softness o'er my heart doth come,
   Linking thy memory with these;
For if, amid those orbs, that roll,
   Thou hast at times a thought of me,
For every one, that stirs thy soul,
   A thousand stir my own of thee.

Even now thy dear remembered eyes,
   Filled up with floods of radiant light,
Seem bending from the twilight skies,
   Outshining all the stars of night;
And thy young face, divinely fair,
   Like a bright cloud seems melting through,
While low sweet whispers fill the air,
   Making my own lips whisper too;
For never does .the soft south wind
   Steal o'er the hushed and lonely sea,
But it awakens in my mind
   A thousand memories of thee.

O! could I,—while these hours of dreams
   Are gathering o'er the silent hills,
While every breeze a minstrel seems,
   And every leaf a harp, that thrills—
Steal all unseen to some hushed place,
   And kneeling 'neath those burning orbs,
Forever gaze on thy sweet face
   Till seeing every sense absorbs,

And, singling out each blessed even
    The star that earliest lights the sea,
Forget another shines in heaven
    While shines the one beloved by thee!

Lost one! companion of the blessed!
    Thou who in purer air dost dwell,
Ere froze the life-drops in thy breast,
    Or fled thy soul its mystic cell,
We passed on earth such hours of bliss
    As none but kindred hearts can know,
And, happy in a world like this,
    But dreamed of that to which we go,
Till thou wert called in thy young years
    To wander o'er that shoreless sea,
Where, like a mist, Time disappears,
    Melting into Eternity.

I'm thinking of some sunny hours,
    That shone out goldenly in June,
When birds were singing 'mong the flowers
    With wild sweet voices all in tune;

When o'er thy locks of paly gold
    Flowed thy transparent veil away,
Till 'neath each snow-white trembling fold
    The Eden of thy bosom lay;
And sheltered 'neath its dark-fringed lid,
    Till raised from thence in girlish glee,
How modestly thy glance lay hid
    From the fond glances bent on thee.

There are some hours, that pass so soon,
    Our spell-touched hearts scarce know they end
And so it was with that sweet June,
    Ere thou wert lost, my gentle friend!
O! how I'll watch each flower that closes
    Through autumn's soft and breezy reign,
Till summer-blooms restore the roses,
    And merry June shall come again!
But, ah! while float its sunny hours
    O'er fragrant shore and trembling sea,
Missing thy face among the flowers,
    How my full heart will mourn for thee!

MY SISTERS.

Like flowers that softly bloom together
   Upon one fair and fragile stem,
Mingling their sweets in sunny weather
   Ere strange rude hands have parted them,
So were we linked unto each other,
   Sweet Sisters, in our childish hours,
For then one fond and gentle mother
   To us was like the stem to flowers;
She was the golden thread, that bound us
   In one bright chain together here,
Till Death unloosed the cord around us,
   And we were severed far and near.

The floweret's stem, when broke or shattered,
   Must cast its blossoms to the wind,
Yet, round the buds, though widely scattered,
   The same soft perfume still we find ;
And thus, although the tie is broken,
   That linked us round our mother's knee,
The memory of words we've spoken,
   When we were children light and free,
Will, like the perfume of each blossom,
   Live in our hearts where'er we roam,
As when we slept on one fond bosom,
   And dwelt within one happy home.

I know that changes have come o'er us;
   Sweet Sisters! we are not the same,
For different paths now lie before us,
   And all three have a different name ;
And yet, if sorrow's dimming fingers
   Have shadowed o'er each youthful brow,
So much of light around them lingers
   I cannot trace those shadows now.

Ye both have those, who love ye only,
   Whose dearest hopes are round you thrown,
While, like a stream that wanders lonely,
   Am I, the youngest, wildest one.

My heart is like the wind, that beareth
   Sweet scents upon its unseen wing—
The wind! that for no creature careth,
   Yet stealeth sweets from every thing:
It hath rich thoughts forever leaping
   Up, like the waves of flashing seas,
That with their music still are keeping
   Soft time with every fitful breeze;
Each leaf that in the bright air quivers,
   The sounds from hidden solitudes,
And the deep flow of far-off rivers,
   And the loud rush of many floods;
All these, and more, stir in my bosom
   Feelings that make my spirit glad,
Like dew-drops shaken in a blossom;
   And, yet there is a something sad

MY SISTERS.

Mixed with those thoughts, like clouds, that hover
  Above us in the quiet air,
Veiling the moon's pale beauty over,
  Like a dark spirit brooding there.

But, Sisters! those wild thoughts were never
  Yours! ye would not love, like me,
To gaze upon the stars forever,
  To hear the wind's wild melody.
Ye'd rather look on smiling faces,
  And linger round a cheerful hearth,
Than mark the stars' bright hiding-places
  As they peep out upon the earth.
But, Sisters! as the stars of even
  Shrink from day's golden flashing eye,
And, melting in the depths of heaven,
  Veil their soft beams within the sky:
So shall we pass, the joyous-hearted,
  The fond, the young, like stars that wane,
Till every link of earth be parted,
  To form in heaven *one mystic chain.*

THE FIRST DEATH OF THE HOUSEHOLD.

O ! MANY a mournful year hath flown
   Since first amid our family-band
Death came and stole our loveliest one,
   And bore her to the spirit-land;
Yet shrined with many a sweet sad thought,
   That loved one's memory lingers still,
For O! she left a void, that naught
   But mournful thoughts could fill.

Years have passed by, I said, and yet
   It only seems the other day,
Since round her dying bed we met
   With breaking hearts to weep and pray.

FIRST DEATH OF THE HOUSEHOLD.

Her gentle soul we strove to think
    Would linger yet 'mid earthly flowers,
Even when 'twas trembling on the brink
    Of lovelier worlds than ours.

Yes! there e'en when all hope had flown,
    We wept away each lingering hour,
Until the shades of death came down
    And closed at last the shutting flower;
And yet it seemed like sin to grieve
    For one so patient and resigned;
For, if she mourned, 'twas but to leave
    Such breaking hearts behind.

She died—yet death could scarcely chill
    Her smiling beauties, though she lay
With cold extended limbs, for still
    Her face looked fairer than the day.
Those eyes, once eloquent with bliss,
    Were closed as soft as shutting flowers.
O! few could bear a sight like this,
    Yet such a sight was ours.

FIRST DEATH OF THE HOUSEHOLD.

How slowly wore that long, long day!
   Like spirits in some haunted place
We'd sit and sigh, then steal away
   To look once more on that pale face·
We could not think her soul had passed
   The awful bounds of mortal strife,
That the warm heart was cold at last
   That loved us more than life.

And when the funeral rite was said,
   They bore her from our happy home
And left her with the silent dead,
   A pale-faced tenant of the tomb;
They reared no marble 'mid the flowers
   Above her grave to mark the spot,
Ye· many a heart as fond as ours
   Still holds her unforgot.

Months passed, yet still our sorrow gushed,
   The free glad laugh no more was heard,
And many a little voice was hushed,
   That used to warble like a bird.

And though at times we strove to smile
  Serenely for each other's sake,
We wept in secret all the while
  As if our hearts would break.

Yet why should death be linked with fear?
  A single breath, a low-drawn sigh,
Can break the ties that bind us here,
  And waft the spirit to the sky.
Such was her end, a calm release,
  No clingings to this mortal clod;
She closed her eyes, and stood in peace
  Before a smiling God.

THE MAIDEN'S FIRST LOVE.

Her dove-like spirit through her mournful eyes
Looks softly upward to its native heaven;
For a love-spell upon her being lies,
Whose many mystic links may not be riven.
Love breathed into her girlish heart, perchance,
On some sweet eve, beside a pleasant stream,
Poured from the lightning of a radiant glance,
Till love's wild passion kindled passion's dream.

For love at first is but a dreamy thing,
That slyly nestles in the human heart,
A morning lark, that never plumes its wing
Till hopes and fears, like lights and shadows, part:

THE MAIDEN'S FIRST LOVE

And thus unconscious as she looks above
She breathes his blessed name in murmurs low,
Yet never for a moment thinks of love,
And almost wonders why she murmurs so.

Ah! mournful one! the thoughts thou wilt not speak,
Their trembling music at thy heart-strings play,
Till the bright blood, that mantles to thy cheek,
In faint and fainter blushes melts away.
Thine is the mournful joy, that in the dawn
Of early love upon the spirit broods,
Till the young heart, grown timid as a fawn,
Seeks the still starlight and the shadowy woods.

Yes, by the chastened light of those soft eyes,
That never swam in sorrowing tears before,
By the low breathing of those mournful sighs,
That, like a mist-wreath, cloud thy spirit o'er,
And by the color that doth come and go,
Making more lovely thy bewildering charms—
Maiden! 'tis love that fills thy breast of snow,
Heaving with tender fears and soft alarms.

My bosom trembles at the love intense,
Breathed eloquently from thine earnest eyes,
The love that is to thee a new-born sense,
Waking sweet thoughts and gentle sympathies;
O! for the sake of all thou wert, and art,
May Love's soft Eden-winds, that seem to kiss
The very foldings of thy love-toned heart,
Be but the prelude to some deeper bliss.

THE STARS.

YE snow-white clouds, whose fleecy wings enfold
  The stars, that light yon boundless breadth of blue,
Roll back your edges, tinged with deepest gold,
  And softly let the peaceful wanderers through,
Till, one by one, they burst upon my eyes,
O'ertaking my young heart with sudden sweet surprise.

Celestial lights, lit by the power divine,
  That bids you roll through yonder azure plain,
Ye startle thoughts within this heart of mine,
  That I must breathe, or it will break in twain!
Companions of the twilight and the dew,
Smile on the Minstrel-girl, who strings her harp anew.

THE STARS

I am not one whose eagle-eye can reach
   The mystic things, within your golden spheres,
Yet better thoughts than science'e'er can teach
   Are softly brimming my young eyes with tears;
For e'en the simplest heart at times may scan
What years can scarce unfold, or wisdom teach to man

How oft, when but a child, in wildest glee,
   I've climbed the summit of some breezy hill,
Whose mossy sides went sloping to the sea
   Where slept another heaven serenely still,
While, from the mighty stronghold of the seas,
The dead sent up their dirge upon the twilight breeze.

And there beneath a fringe of dewy leaves,
   That drooped away from many a bended bough,
I used to lie on summer's golden eves,
   And gaze above as I am gazing now,
Thinking each lustrous star a heavenly shrine
For an immortal soul, and wondered which was mine.

But now the moon, beside yon lonely hill,
   Lifts high her trembling cup of paly gold,
And all the planets, following slow and still,
   Along the deep their solemn marches hold,
While here and there some meteor's startling ray
Shoots streaks of arrowy fire far down the milky-way

The milky-way! ah! fair, illumined path,
   That leadest upward to the gate of heaven,
My spirit, soaring from this world of scath,
   Is lost with thee amid the clouds of even,
And there, upborne on Fancy's glittering wing,
Floats by the golden gate, and hears the angels sing.

O! who can lift above a careless look,
   While such bright scenes as these his thoughts engage,
And doubt, while reading from so fair a book,
   That God's own finger traced the glowing page,
Or deem the radiance of yon blue expanse,
With all its starry hosts, the careless work of Chance?

THE STARS.

O blessed stars! whene'er ye softly fling
   A silvery trembling down by lake and hill,
'Tis then that sweet Religion's holy wing
   Broods o'er the spirit, and doth softly fill
Its silent depths with that pure heavenly bliss,
That we so seldom feel, save at an hour like this.

For ne'er since love's sweet raptures o'er me stole,
   As first its young existence dawned in sighs,
Have I e'er felt such fulness in my soul,
   Such depth of softness at my heart and eyes,
As I now feel upon this dewy sod,
Pondering with holy awe the wondrous works of God

Ye bring the time when happy lovers meet
   In some lone spot, when not a sound is heard
Save their own sighs, or the unequal beat
   Of their young hearts to tender wishes stirred,
As hand seeks hand, and meeting glances tell
The unuttered tale of love, too sweetly and too well-

But all in vain to thought's tumultuous flow
   I strive to give the strength of glowing words;
The waves of feeling, tossing to and fro
   In broken music o'er my harp's loose chords,
Give but their fainting echoes from my soul,
As through its silent depths their wild swift currents roll.

Yet, thou, who art mine inspiration, thou,
   For whose sweet praises still I strive to sing,
I will not murmur once, when, bending low,
   At thy dear feet my broken harp I fling,
Well pleased if others think this song I send,
Though all unworthy praise, too simple to offend.

STANZAS

Pale star, that, with thy soft sad light,
    Came out upon my bridal eve,
I have a song to sing to-night
    Before thou tak'st thy mournful leave.
Since then, so softly time hath stirred,
    That months have almost seemed like hours,
And I am like some little bird,
    That's slept too long among the flowers,
And, waking, sits with waveless wing,
    Soft-singing, 'mid the shades of even;
But O! with sadder heart I sing—
    I sing of one who dwells in heaven.

The winds are soft, the clouds are few,
   And tenderest thought my heart beguiles,
As, floating up through mist and dew,
   The pale young moon comes out and smiles;
And to the green resounding shore,
   In silvery troops the ripples crowd,
Till all the ocean, dimpled o'er,
   Lifts up its voice and laughs aloud:
And star on star, all soft and calm,
   Floats up yon arch serenely blue,
And lost to earth, and steeped in balm,
   My spirit floats in ether too.

Loved one! though lost to human sight,
   I feel thy spirit lingering near,
As softly as I feel the light
   That trembles through the atmosphere;
As in some temple's holy shades,
   Though mute the hymn, and hushed the prayer,
A solemn awe the soul pervades,
   Which tells that worship has been there;

STANZAS.

A breath of incense left alone,
  Where many a censer swung around,
Will thrill the wanderer like a tone,
  Who treads on consecrated ground.

I know thy soul, from worlds of bliss,
  That stoops awhile to dwell with me,
Hath caught the prayer I breathed in this,
  That I at last might dwell with thee.
I hear a murmur from the seas
  That thrills me like thy spirit's sighs;
I hear a voice on every breeze;
  That makes to mine its low replies—
A voice, all low and sweet, like thine,
  It gives an answer to my prayer,
And brings my soul from heaven a sign
  That it shall know and meet thee there.

I'll know thee there by that sweet face,
  Round which a tender halo plays,
Still touched with that expressive grace
  That made thee lovely all thy days;

STANZAS.

By that sweet smile, that o'er it shed
    A beauty like the light of even,
Whose soft expression never fled,
    Even when its soul had flown to heaven;
I'll know thee by the starry crown,
    That glitters in thy golden hair:
O! by these blessed signs alone
    I'll know thee there—I'll know thee there.

For thy soft eye, within whose sphere,
    The sweets of youth and beauty met,
That swam in love and softness here,
    Must swim in love and softness yet;
For O! its dark and liquid beams,
    Though saddened by a thousand sighs,
Were holier than the light that streams
    Down from the gates of paradise—
Were bright and radiant like the morn,
    Yet soft and dewy as the eve—
Too sad for eyes where smiles are born—
    Too young for eyes that learn to grieve.

I wonder if this cool, sweet breeze
   Hath touched thy lips and fanned thy brow;
For all my spirit hears and sees
   Recalls thee to my memory now:
For every hour we breathe apart
   Will but increase, if that can be,
The love that fills this mournful heart,
   Already filled so full of thee;
Yet many a tear these eyes must weep,
   And many a sin must be forgiven,
Ere these pale lids shall sink to sleep—
   Ere thou and I shall meet in heaven.

TIME.

ALL hail, thou viewless one, whose lonely wings
  Sweep o'er the earth, unwearied and sublime!
Mysterious agent of the King of kings,
  Whom conquerors obey, and man calls Time!
Compared with thee, even centuries in their might
  Seem but like atoms in the sun's broad ray;
Thou sweep'st them on in thy majestic flight,
  Scattering them from thy plumes like drops of spray
  Cast from the ocean in its scornful play.

Shrined as thou art in my sublimest thought,
  How shall my spirit hail thee? O'er the earth
Thou, with ten thousand worlds that sprang from naught,
  Began'st thy wanderings at creation's birth!
Musing on thee, the expanding spirit, filled

With thoughts too vast for human eloquence,
Shrinks trembling, like a woman's heart when thrilled
   With love's delicious throes—till thought intense
Is lost amid its own magnificence.

Thou floatest imperceptible to sight,
   God-like, diffusing life and death around;
Swift stars shoot round thee in thy rapid flight,
   Dropping like gems from midnight's blue profound;
Swept on with thee, through vast immensity,
   Each blazing sphere in its swift course revolves,
The sunny streams go singing to the sea,
   And the blue wave upon the beach dissolves
     Like woman's hopes, and manhood's high resolves.

Even every heart-beat in the bosom's cell
   Steals o'er the spirit like a funeral toll;
Each solemn stroke is like a passing-bell,
   Heard 'mid the hushes of the startled soul.
The waves of feeling, tossing to and fro
   Like ocean-billows restless and sublime,
The crimson life-drops as they ebb and flow,

TIME.

And the quick pulse with its unequal chime,
All beat with muffled strokes the march of Time.

Each year, that seems so long to us, to thee
   Is but one sweep of thy majestic plume,
Bearing pale millions to the eternal sea,
   Through the dim pathway of the midnight tomb;
Thou touch'st the young and beautiful, and lo!
   Gone are the charms thou never can'st restore,
The fair and glossy tress turns white as snow,
   And the young voice, that warbles o'er and o'er,
Drops its low bird-like note, and sings no more.

Yet, in the rosy dawn of childhood's day,
   How swift the joyous moments seem to flee!
They waft themselves like happy thoughts away,
   Or melt like snow-flakes dropping on the sea;
'Tis pastime then to laugh away the hours,
   That lightly mingle in thy circling race,
Like dancing-girls, all linked with wreaths of flowers,
   Or like swift ripples, that each other chase,
   Or deepening dimples o'er a laughing face.

THE FREED BIRD.

Thy cage is opened, bird! too well I love thee
    To bar the sunny things of earth from thee;
A whole broad heaven of blue lies calm above thee,
    The green-wood waves beneath, and thou art free;
These slender wires shall prison thee no more—
Up, bird! and 'mid the clouds thy thrilling music pour.

Away! away! the laughing waters, playing,
    Break on the fragrant shore in ripples blue,
And the green leaves unto the breeze are laying
    Their shining edges, fringed with drops of dew;
And, here and there, a wild flower lifts its head
Refreshed with sudden life from many a sunbeam shed.

THE FREED BIRD.

How sweet thy voice will sound! for o'er yon river
    The wing of silence, like a dream, is laid,
And naught is heard save where the wood-boughs quiver,
    Making rich spots of trembling light and shade.
And a new rapture thy wild spirit fills,
For joy is on the breeze, and morn upon tne hills.

Now, like the aspen, plays each quivering feather
    Of thy swift pinion, bearing thee along,
Up, where the morning stars once sang together,
    To pour the fulness of thine own rich song;
And now thou'rt mirrored to my dazzled view,
A little dusky speck amid a world of blue.

Yet I will shade mine eye and still pursue thee,
    As thou dost melt in soft ethereal air,
Till angel-ones, sweet bird, will bend to view thee,
    And cease their hymns awhile thine own to share;
And there thou art, with light clouds round thee furled,
Just poised beneath yon vault, that arches o'er the world.

THE FREED BIRD.

A free wild spirit unto thee is given,
    Bright minstrel of the blue celestial dome!
For thou wilt wander to yon upper heaven,
    And bathe thy plumage in the sunbeam's home;
And, soaring upward from thy dizzy height
On free and fearless wing, be lost to human sight.

Lute of the summer clouds! whilst thou art singing
    Unto thy Maker thy soft matin hymn,
My own mild spirit, from its temple springing,
    Would freely join thee in the distance dim;
But I can only gaze on thee and sigh
With heart upon my lip, bright minstrel of the sky!

And yet, sweet bird! bright thoughts to me are given
    As many as the clustering leaves of June;
And my young heart is like a harp of heaven,
    Forever strung unto some pleasant tune;
And my soul burns with wild poetic fire,
Though simple are my strains, and simpler still my lyre

And now, farewell! the wild wind of the mountain
   And the blue streams alone my strains have heard;
And it is well, for from my heart's deep fountain
   They flow, uncultured, as thine own, sweet bird!
For my free thoughts have ever spurned control,
Since this heart held a wish, and this frail form a soul!

THE CAPTIVE SAILOR BOY

The light of many stars
Quivers in tremulous softness on the air,
And the night-breeze is singing here and there,
    Yet from my prison-bars
A narrow strip of sky is all I see—
O! that some kindly hand would set me free!

The bright new moon is hung
Up 'mid the softness of the fleecy clouds,
And the far ocean 'neath its foamy shrouds
    Thrills like a harp fresh strung,
And the wild sea-birds on quick pinions flee—
O! for one glance upon the deep blue sea!

Why should the young and brave
Be fetteι ed thus upon the fresh green earth?
Give me one hour beside my mother's hearth,
    And then for ocean's wave!
Free as the laughing billows I would toss—
O! for the swift wing of the albatros!

When slumber waves her wand
Over my brow, I wander in my dreams
Close by the ripples of our soft blue streams
    Far in my native land,
And lovely visions o'er my eyelids play—
O! that I could but dream my life away!

I see my mother then;
A pleasant smile sleeps on her features fair,
And the low cadence of her whispered prayer
    Steals on my ear again,
As when I knelt beside her blessed knee—
Mother, sweet Mother, dost thou pray for me?

THE CAPTIVE SAILOR BOY.

Upon the summer rose
Nature's faint pencillings are softly seen,
Laid on with cunning hand, and bright and green,
　　Where the wood-branches close
The honey-suckle wreathes our cottage eaves—
Alas! I may not sit beneath its leaves!

Before I sought the sea,
I used to wander with my sister sweet,
And many a winding path our little feet
　　Made round the old oak tree,
Where in the sunshine we were wont to play—
And they are there—but I am far away!

O! could I only ride
Upon the ocean where the wild winds meet,
And where the sea-shell singeth passing sweet
　　Under the trembling tide,
The demon of the storms I would not fear—
But O! I am a fettered captive here!

THE CAPTIVE SAILOR BOY.

O ! could I see my home
If but to kiss my sister's cheek once more,
And hear thee, Mother, bless me o'er and o'er !
    For then not e'en my doom
Could dim thy truant's laughter-loving eye—
Alas ! without thy blessing I must die !

    Die in this dreary cell,
With no fond ear to catch my parting breath ;
In bondage I must wrestle here with death,
    Without one sweet farewell
From lips that oft have smiled on me in joy—
Alas ! sweet Mother, for thy captive boy !

THE GOLDEN RINGLET.

Here is a little golden tress
    Of soft unbraided hair,
The all that's left of loveliness,
    That once was thought so fair;
And yet though time hath dimmed its sheen,
    Though all beside hath fled,
I hold it here, a link between
    My spirit and the dead.

Yes! from this shining ringlet still
    A mournful memory springs,
That melts my heart and sends a thrill
    Through all its trembling strings.

THE GOLDEN RINGLET.

I think of her, the loved, the wept,
    Upon whose forehead fair,
For eighteen years, like sunshine, slept
    This golden curl of hair.

O sunny tress! the joyous brow,
    Where thou didst lightly wave,
With all thy sister-tresses now
    Lies cold within the grave;
That cheek is of its bloom bereft,
    That eye no more is gay;
Of all her beauties thou art left,
    A solitary ray.

Four years have passed, this very June,
    Since last we fondly met—
Four years! and yet it seems too soon
    To let the heart forget—
Too soon to let that lovely face
    From our sad thoughts depart,
And to another give the place
    She held within the heart.

Her memory still within my mind
  Retains its sweetest power:
It is the perfume left behind
  To whisper of the flower;
Each blossom, that in moments gone
  Bound up this sunny curl,
Recalls the form, the look, the tone
  Of that enchanting girl.

Her step was like an April rain
  O'er beds of violets flung,
Her voice the prelude to a strain
  Before the song is sung;
Her life—'twas like a half-blown flower
  Closed ere the shades of even,
Her death, the dawn, the blushing hour,
  That opes the gate of heaven.

A single tress! how slight a thing
  To sway such magic art,
And bid each soft remembrance spring
  Like blossoms in the heart!

It leads me back to days of old,
 To her I loved so long,
Whose locks outshone pellucid gold,
 Whose lips o'erflowed with song.

Since then I've heard a thousand lays
 From lips as sweet as hers,
Yet when I strove to give them praise,
 I only gave them tears;
I could not bear, amid the throng
 Where jest and laughter rung,
To hear another sing the song
 That trembled on her tongue.

A single shining tress of hair
 To bid such memories start!
But tears are on its lustre—there
 I lay it on my heart:
O! when in Death's cold arms I sink,
 Who then, with gentle care,
Will keep for me a dark-brown link—
 A ringlet of my hair?

THE COTTAGE BAND.

I know a neat white cot, that peeps out brightly
From its repose amid green wavy trees,
    That murmur to the breeze,
Round which young feet are heard to fall as lightly
As summer rain-drops on the sighing rose,
    Lulling it to repose.

There, when the joyous lark is upward springing,
With his sweet song to greet the early morn,
    Unto the ear is borne
The silvery laugh of childhood, wildly ringing
Upon the stillness of the soft blue air,
    For happy hearts are there:

THE COTTAGE BAND.

Hearts that are filled from love's eternal fountain
Till each is like a deep o'erflowing well,
    Or a wild floweret's bell,
Hid 'neath the brow of some o'erhanging mountain,
Giving its perfume to each wind it meets,
    Yet losing not its sweets.

And there at noontide, mid the trembling glances
Of the sweet starry jasmine gleaming out,
    Is heard a young boy's shout,
Clear as the singing of a stream, that dances
Unto the breeze in all its boundless glee—
    As clear, but O! more free.

And near his side a fairy creature lingers,
His little sister with her moss-rose cheek,
    And eye so softly meek,
Parting the clustering vines with dimpled fingers,
And seizing from their long and wiry stems,
    Their pale and quivering gems.

And there at eve, beneath the starlight gleamings,
Sits their young mother in soft pensive grace,
    With sweetly smiling face,
Hushing her babe unto its heavenly dreamings,
And, with bent listening ear and graceful head,
    Waiting her husband's tread.

And, when his step is heard among the flowers,
Sweet lips are wreathed in smiles, and ready feet
    Fly forth his own to meet;
And the calm stillness of the twilight hours
Is broken by soft whispered words of love,
    Stirring the air above.

And this is all! yet oft my fancy painteth
That quiet lovely spot unto my view,
    Where the warm sun looks through
The leafy boughs, and where the white rose fainteth
Upon the breeze, that oft its leaves hath fanned—
    Blessed be that cottage-band!

THE LITTLE STEP-SON.

I have a little step-son, the loveliest thing alive :
A noble sturdy boy is he, and yet he's only five ;
His smooth cheek hath a blooming glow, his eyes are black as jet
And his lips are like two rose-buds, all tremulous and wet :
His days pass off in sunshine, in laughter, and in song,
As careless as a summer rill, that sings itself along ;
For like a pretty fairy tale, that's all too quickly told,
Is the young life of a l ttle one, that's only five years old.

He's dreaming on his happy couch before the day grows dark,
He's up with morning's rosy ray a-singing with the lark ;
Where'er the flowers are freshest, where'er the grass is green,
Witn light locks waving on the wind his fairy form is seen,

THE LITTLE STEP-SON.

Amid the whistling March winds, amid the April showers ;
He warbles with the singing birds and blossoms with the flowers ;
He cares not for the summer heat, he cares not for the cold—
My sturdy little step-son, that's only five years old.

How touching 'tis to see him clasp his dimpled hands in prayer,
And raise his little rosy face with reverential air !
How simple is his eloquence ! how soft his accents fall,
When pleading with the King of kings to love and bless us all ;
And when from prayer he bounds away in innocence and joy,
The blessing of a smiling God goes with the sinless boy ;
A little lambkin of the flock, within the Saviour's fold,
Is he my lovely step-son, that's only five years old.

I have not told you of our home, that in the summer hours,
Stands in its simple modesty half hid among the flowers ;
I have not said a single word about our mines of wealth—
Our treasures are this little boy, contentment, peace, and health ;
For even a lordly hall to us would be a voiceless place
Without the gush of his glad voice, the gleams of his bright face ;
And many a courtly pair, I ween, would give their gems and gold
For a noble happy boy like ours, some four or five years old.

TO A HUMMING-BIRD.

A MERRY welcome to thee, glittering bird!
Lover of summer flowers and sunny things!
A night hath passed since my young buds have heard
The music of thy rainbow-colored wings—
Wings, that flash sparkles out where'er they quiver,
Like sudden sunlight rushing o'er a river.

A merry welcome and a treat for thee!
Here are fresh blossoms opening bright and new,
Ready to yield thee, for thy melody,
Their first rich sighs and drops of honey-dew,
Opening their blushing petals to the glances
Of silvery sheen, that round thy light form dances.

TO A HUMMING-BIRD.

Methinks thou'rt early out—the queenly night
    Her star-gemmed curtain scarce has folded back;
And now the glorious sun, a monarch bright,
    Bursts forth into his gold-pavilioned track,
Kissing from dew-bent flowers the tears of even,
And scattering the bright mists from earth and heaven

How fair is all around! and thou, bright thing,
    Though but a speck, a brilliant one thou art;
I almost think the humming of thy wing
    Must be the merry echoes of thy heart;
For what if other birds have happier voices?
Thou need'st not care—thy very wing rejoices.

Child of the sunshine! bird of summer hours!
    Brief is thy life, yet happy as 'tis brief,
For thou wilt pass away when bloom-touched flowers
    Are fading from the green earth, leaf by leaf;
I envy thee, for when the things we cherish
Are withering round, 'tis meet with them to perish.

Here thou mayst banquet till the first faint gleams
 Of twilight wander o'er the face of day,
Wooing our spirits to the land of dreams;
 Then on a sunbeam thou wilt flit away;
But, at the earliest dawn of morning's hour,
I'll welcome thee again unto my bower.

THE BROKEN-HEARTED.

SHE faded slowly mid unwithering roses;
   In the first flush of youth, her heart had been
Bright as a full bud when it first discloses
   Its summer tints beneath its hood of green;
For there was one to whom her heart she'd given,
   Yet she had won no vow of love from him,
And shadows gathered o'er her sunny heaven
   Till e'en the lingering star of hope grew dim.

Life had to her been sweet as music measures,
   That steal forth from a lute on some faint breeze,
And her sweet thoughts were like uncounted treasures,
   That cluster in the depths of trembling seas;

There played around her lip a smile so winning,
    And in her eye there shone such tenderness,
That none could look on her and dream of sinning,
    She was so pure in virgin loveliness.

'Twas when soft summer winds were lightly stirring,
    One golden eve in bright midsummer time,
That first, with honeyed words and looks endearing,
    He stole within her path in manhood's prime;
And when sweet jasmine vines their wreaths were looping
    Around her bower, beneath their fragrant shade
With her fair head upon his bosom drooping,
    She'd list entranced to all the loved one said.

And at the hour, when silvery dew-drops slumbered
    Upon the whispering grass and young rose-leaves,
With restless heart each quiet star she numbered,
    For he would seek her side at starry eves;
And though beneath his glance her heart would quiver,
    And her voice, when to him she spoke or sung,
Seemed like the sad moan of a low-voiced river,
    Still in his presence tremblingly she hung.

But when she found he loved her as a brother
    Would love a gentle sister, with deep art
She tried each wild and wayward thought to smother,
    But 'twas a bitter task—it broke her heart;
For, though her red lips woke a strain of gladness,
    A tear into her hazel eye would spring,
And in its depths there shone a dreamy sadness,
    That told of deep distress and sorrowing.

But, when far, far away o'er dell and mountain,
    He left her side to seek a distant land,
Love still hung weeping over Memory's fountain,
    And her young brow drooped on her pale thin hand;
And when the peeping flowers of spring were wreathing,
    And the soft air was burdened with perfume,
Life's last sad music on her lip was breathing,
    And she was lightly gathered to the tomb.

THE YOUNG LOVERS.

SHE was a witching creature, o'er whose head
　　Scarce eighteen summers on bright wings had flown,
Into whose spirit poetry had shed
　　Her sweetest odors, breathed fresh from her own ;
Pure modesty around her light form spread
　　Her spotless drapery, and, like a zone,
Beauty encircled her, for her wild glances
Spell-bound all hearts in sweet bewildering trances.

Her beauty was of a mysterious kind,
　　Baffling the pencil, that its charms would trace,
For the rich depths of her illumined mind
　　Such flitting gleams gave to her love-toned face,

That the spell-taken eye could ever find
　Some charm unseen before; a willowy grace
Played in the movements of her form, just moulded
Into soft roundness, like a rose unfolded.

Her step was lighter than the wanton breeze,
　That breathes its love-sighs to the dreamy hours
And graceful as light vapors o'er the seas,
　Melting away in soft and dewy showers,
While, with a simple grace and natural ease,
　She half reclined upon a bed of flowers,
And o'er her shoulder, rainbow like, there bended
A youth, whose sighs with her warm breathings blended.

He was a being e'en more glorious still;
　The seal of genius on his brow was seen,
With thoughts bright as the dews that flowers distil,
　When leaves dance in the starlight fresh and green;
His was a voice rich as a harp's deep thrill,
　A large dark eagle-eye, and noble mien,
Yet with a heart so tuned to softest measures,
His very face beamed forth bewildering pleasures.

THE YOUNG LOVERS.

As o'er her drooping form he softly bent,
    The pressure of his lip was on her brow,
While to her cheek the warm blood came and went,
    Varying each moment with her rich thoughts' flow,
For each, within her heaving bosom pent,
    Seemed struggling on her up-turned face to glow,
While tell-tale dimples, in her cheeks appearing,
Told that a sweet love-thought her heart was stirring.

For closely round that young and happy pair
    Passion had wove her softest, sweetest ties,
While, like two spirits fresh from heaven, there
    They sat beneath their own blue native skies,
He playing with some stray tress of her hair
    And gazing mutely in her melting eyes,
While from their glowing glances both were drinking
The passionate love that in their hearts was sinking.

THE BLIND GIRL'S LAMENT.

I sit beneath the grape-vine, that o'ercreepeth
   The humble arch above our cottage door,
While on its purple clusters softly sleepeth
   The holy radiance that the moonbeams pour
The joyous song-bird in the starlight singeth
   Unto the dreaming buds its vesper hymn,
But not a single ray of gladness springeth
   Within my heart—alas! my eye is dim.

I know the hour when silent-footed even
   Puts on her shadowy mantle light and fair,
When, as she waves her wand o'er earth and heaven,
   The stars float up within the soft blue air;

'Tis then I fling aside my long loose tresses
  Unto the kisses of the wanton wind,
And strive to sing and smile, but ah! there presses
  A gloomy pall upon me—I am blind.

O! could I steal forth, when the daylight fadeth
  From rock and tree, to greet the summer eves,
To watch the primrose, that from sunlight shadeth
  Its golden cup, unfold its twilight leaves,
To lay my warm brow to the breeze that wooeth
  The wild sea-ripples to the sounding shore—
The soft south breeze that perfume round us streweth—
  But ah! 'tis vain—my eye is shaded o'er.

My little sister often softly layeth
  Her velvet cheek to mine, and bids me go
Where the young moss-rose its soft bloom displayeth,
  And the wild daisies in their brightness glow;
I hear her small feet as she lightly dances
  Like a winged fairy o'er the emerald grass,
She thinks not of her sister's clouded glances,
  For where she trips the blind girl may not pass.

THE BLIND GIRL'S LAMENT.

When my young brother in his beauty boundeth
    Up with the lark to greet the morning sky,
While through the forest-aisles his laugh resoundeth,
    The tear-drops gather to my darkened eye;
And when, with rosy cheek and bright eye burning,
    He seeks my side in all his boyish glee,
My heart is troubled with a secret yearning
    To meet his glance—but ah! I cannot see.

My meek fond mother tells me I am brighter
    Than the sweet flowers she twines amid my hair;
She thinks her praise will make my spirit lighter,
    But O! I pine not to be bright or fair;
I may be lovelier than the violet flower,
    That shines, they say, beneath its broad leaves hid,
But beauty is to me a worthless dower,
    While darkly rolls mine eye beneath its lid.

I cannot gaze upon their pleasant faces,
    Where the soft light of beauty ever beams,
Yet on my mind their fair forms Fancy traces,
    And their deep looks pierce through my nightly dreams;

THE BLIND GIRL'S LAMENT.

I feel my mother's soft eye as it flashes
    Like a lone star that looks down from the sky,
Trembling so softly 'neath its silky lashes,
    Yet, when I wake, 'tis with a darkened eye.

Ah! little know they of the dreamy sadness
    That shadows o'er my spirit's viewless urn,
For they can look out on the free world's gladness,
    Where blossoms blow, and stars shoot out and burn,
While I must sit, a fair yet darkened flower,
    Amid the bright band gathered round our hearth,
The only sad thing in our sweet home bower—
    O! for one glance upon the fresh green earth!

TO ———.

Wilt thou not think of me with mournful heart,
When our warm lips and clasping hands shall part?
    And in thy soul's deep cell
Will not my memory be treasured up,
Fresh as the dews that in the lily's cup
    In sweetness dwell?

And, as those dropping dews upon the flowers
Sweeten their leaves through all the dreamy hours
    When weary eyelids close,
So may my memory, in thine hours of gloom,
Be to thy soul a balm, a soft perfume,
    To soothe thy woes.

TO ———.

I'd have thee think of me when thou art gone,
As one round whom a fairy spell is thrown
    Of bright poetic dreams,
Whose sweet wild thoughts, from their unfathomed fount,
The heart, like flashing waters, upward mount
    In sparkling gleams.

And, when thy wandering feet are roaming o'er
The golden sands of some bright, distant shore,
    Where the soft-chanting waves
Murmur their dirge-like music low and deep
Over the depths where wild, wild spirits sleep
    In their dark caves—

Then think of her whose heart, 'mid scenes like these,
Would thrill and echo to each passing breeze
    And to the water's chime—
Into whose eyes unbidden tears would rush,
Till from her heart her feelings all would gush
    In untaught rhyme.

TO ———.

And when Night spreads o'er all her sable shroud,
The time when sweet emotions softly crowd
    Within the human breast,
Will not the memory of these thoughts of love,
Scarce owned by us, yet registered above,
    Make thee more blessed!

By the love-links that round our young hearts wreathe,
By all we feel, but cannot, dare not breathe,
    Whate'er may be our lot,
And by thy fond glance melting into mine,
I ask of thee, where'er that glance may shine
    Forget me not!

HE CAME TOO LATE.

He came too late—he came too late
  To soothe her spirit's silent anguish,
So deep her love, so sad her fate,
  So sweetly lost, she seemed to languish;
His gift of love, the ring of gold,
  Had fallen from her wasted finger,
Her lips were pale, where smiles of old,
  In dimpling sweetness, loved to linger;
Yet still she kept his broken vow,
  Still hoarded up his every token;
But death the lone one, claims her now—
  He came too late, her heart was broken.

HE CAME TOO LATE.

I saw her once—her locks of gold,
    Intwined with many a radiant blossom,
Back from her snow-white forehead rolled,
    And floated o'er her swelling bosom.
Around her slight and matchless form
    A thousand graces seemed to hover:
'Twas moulded to a perfect charm,
    Yet pining for a faithless lover:
I passed her by, yet on my ear
    Her bird-like voice came ringing after;
I little thought, a struggling tear
    Was lost amid its silvery laughter.

He came too late—in days of old,
    When by her side he loved to wander,
And time that makes the heart grow cold,
    But served to make his bosom fonder,
That heart, in which he seemed to live,
    Was yielded up with bashful pleasure,
And though 'twas all she had to give,
    That heart was in itself a treasure;

HE CAME TOO LATE.

He left her—'mid the vain and great
    He never found so fair a blossom;
He came at last, but O! too late—
    She slept within her Saviour's bosom

Strange that the love-lorn heart will beat
    With rapture wild amid its folly—
No grief so soft, no pain so sweet
    As love's delicious melancholy.
And thus, though life and hope grew dim,
    She nursed the flame she could not smother;
It seemed more sweet to die for him
    Than live the worshipped of another.
And did Contentment fold its wing
    Around his heart while hers was riven?
No! in his bosom lurked the sting—
    He came, but she had flown to heaven.

He came too late—once, sweetly blessed,
    She reigned amid earth's radiant creatures:
No smiling nymph had e'er possessed
    A fairer form, or lovelier features.

HE CAME TOO LATE.

Joy lit her eye's delighted beam,
  Love dwelt in its impassioned glances
Yet filled it with that heavenly gleam,
  That sweetly awes while it entrances
Yet, as the ring-dove mourns its mate,
  She pined for him the faithless-hearted
He came, but O! he came too late,
  For she, the loved one, had departed.

THE AMERICAN SWORD.

Sword of our gallant fathers, defender of the brave,
Of Washington upon the field and Perry on the wave !
Well might Columbia's foemen beneath thy death-strokes reel,
For each hand was firm that drew thee, and each heart as true
    as steel ;
There's not a tarnish on thy sheen, a rust upon thy blade ;
Though the noble hands that drew thee are in dust and ashes laid;
Thou'rt still the scourge of tyrants, the safeguard of the free,
And may God desert our banner when we surrender thee !

Sword of a thousand victories ! thy splendors led the way,
When our warriors trod the battle-field in terrible array :
Thou wert seen amid the carnage, like an angel in thy wrath ;
The vanquished and the vanquisher bestrewed thy gory path ;

The life-blood of the haughty foe made red the slippery sod
Where thy crimson blade descended like the lightning glance of God!
They poured their ranks like autumn leaves, their life-blood as the sea,
But they battled for a tyrant—we battled to be free!

Sword of a thousand heroes, how holy is thy blade,
So often drawn by Valor's arm, by gentle Pity's stayed!
The warrior breathes his vow by thee, and seals it with a kiss,
He never gives a holier pledge, he asks no more than this;
And, when he girds thee to his side with battle in his face,
He feels within his single arm the strength of all his race;
He shrines thee in his noble breast, with all things bright and free,
And may God desert his standard, when he surrenders thee!

Sword of our country's battles! forever mayst thou prove,
Amid Columbia's freemen, the thunderbolt of Jove;
Where like a youthful victress, with her holy flag unfurled,
She sits amid the nations, the empress of the world.

Behold the heaven-born Goddess, in her glory and increase,
Extending in her lovely hands the olive-branch of peace,
Thy glittering steel is girded on, the safeguard of the free,
And may God desert her standard when she surrenders thee!

VIOLA.

She hath passed like a bird from the minstrel throng,
She has gone to the land where the lovely belong '
Her place is hushed by her lover's side,
Yet his heart is full of his fair young bride;
The hopes of his spirit are crushed and bowed
As he thinks of his love in her long white shroud;
For the fragrant sighs of her perfumed breath
Were kissed from her lips by his rival—Death.

Cold is her bosom, her thin white arms
All mutely crossed o'er its icy charms,
As she lies, like a statue of Grecian art,
With a marble brow and a cold hushed heart.

Her locks were bright, but their gloss is hid,
Her eye is sunk 'neath its waxen lid:
And thus she lies in her narrow hall—
Our fair young minstrel—the loved of all.

Light as a bird's were her springing feet,
Her heart as joyous, her song as sweet;
Yet never again shall that heart be stirred
With its glad wild songs like a singing bird;
Never again shall the strains be sung,
That in sweetness dropped from her silver tongue;
The music is over, and Death's cold dart
Hath broken the spell of that free glad heart.

Often at eve when tne breeze is still,
And the moon floats up by the distant hill,
As I wander alone 'mid the summer bowers,
And wreathe my locks with the sweet wild flowers,
I will think of the time when she lingered there
With her mild blue eyes, and her long fair hair;
I will treasure her name in my bosom-core:
But my heart is sad—I can sing no more.

TO THE EVENING STAR.

If all those bright stars in yon azure-arched heaven
Are the mansions of rest for the pure ones of earth,
I hope I may dwell in yon bright star of even,
For they say that it smiled o'er the place of my birth.

When all the sweet voices are mute that have blessed me,
And my form from the green earth is fading away,
O! then in that pure star how sweetly I'll rest me,
And linger forever within its mild ray.

Soft star, when around me the weary are sleeping,
And all the bright blossoms their velvet leaves close,
If thou art above me thy silent watch keeping,
My bosom is calm as I sink to repose.

TO THE EVENING STAR.

I feel 'neath thy soft beam a holy devotion,
That hushes my light tones of laughter and glee;
Mine eyelids are wet with a tearful emotion,
For my warm heart is melting while gazing on thee.

As the long dreamy hours the lone captive numbers,
From his iron-bound casement he looks on thy beam.
Till, losing his sorrows, he sinks to his slumbers,
While o'er his wild spirit there steals a sweet dream.

When the sailor-boy roams o'er the tempest-tossed ocean,
And thinks of the fond ones he never may see,
He'll murmur a prayer 'mid the billows' commotion
For the loved and the absent, while gazing on thee.

How sweet to my bosom the soothing reflection,
That, should some rude blight all my earthly hopes mar,
From the depths of my heart the pure waves of affection
May gush in their sweetness to thee, gentle star.

TO THE EVENING STAR.

When all the wild faults of my youth are forgiven,
And the light of thy pale beam no longer I see,
And the last earthly link from my spirit is riven,
With an angel's light pinion I'll waft me to thee.

BREATHE NOT A SIGH.

BREATHE not a sigh when we are parting—
    'Tis vain to sigh:
Nor let a single tear be starting
    In thy soft eye.

I know 'tis sad for hearts like ours,
    So warm and true,
To pine for loving smiles, as flowers
    Languish for dew.

Yet I shall have sweet thoughts to cheer me
    When thou art gone,
For, in my dreams, will linger near me
    The absent one.

And, as those dreams at pensive even
    Steal over me,
I'll lift my melting heart to heaven
    In prayer for thee.

Through the deep gloom that darkens o'er thee,
    The star of fame
Shines like a beacon-light before thee—
    Go! win a name.

And then if thou shouldst woo another
    To be thy bride,
Although my thoughts I cannot smother,
    I will not chide.

But shouldst thou hear that grief is paling
    My young cheek's bloom,
That Death my slender form is veiling
    For the dark tomb—

Then let thy lip be softly sighing
    Like a low lute,
Breathing its music o'er the dying
    For sweet lips mute

And when these hands thou'st clasped so often,
    Are cold and chill,
And this warm heart no tone can soften
    To love's sweet thrill—

Then, though light airy forms assemble
    Where thine will be,
I know thy heart will softly tremble
    Still true to me

THE DYING GIRL.

The fitful breeze, that, through the sultry day
Had fanned the fainting blossoms with its breath,
Stole through the open lattice, where there lay
A pale young girl upon the couch of death;
Her glance was fixed upon the moon, that rolled
Through blue and starlight in the vaulted sky,
As if she knew her fleeting hours were told,
And wished to take one lingering look and die.

Beside that humble couch, there dropped one form,
The gentle mother of the dying one,
For grief had bowed her spirit, as the storm
Bends the soft rose upon its emerald throne;
There lay her child, the beautiful, the young,
The breath just sighing on her lip of snow,
And her soft ringlets, all dishevelled, flung
Back from the whiteness of her deathly brow.

Sadly she bent above her; though her look
Was tearless as she sought her daughter's eye.
Yet her lip quivered like a bright leaf, shook
By the strong tempest as it sweeps the sky;
"Daughter!" she murmured, and the maiden turned
Unto her mother's face her mournful glance,
In which life's flickering taper wildly burned,
For she was startled as if from a trance.

And, at that voice so thrilling to her ear,
A thousand tender thoughts her heart oppressed,
Till to her blue eye tear-drop followed tear,
And the white linen heaved above her breast;
About her mother's neck she softly threw
Her pale thin arms, nestling her young head
Within her sheltering bosom, dashed the dew
From her soft cheek, and in low accents said—

 Mother, my hour is come,
The wing of death is o'er me, for my brow
Is damp and chill—sweet mother, I must go
 Down to the silent tomb.

Yet not for this I grieve;
It is to think that I am leaving thee
Poor and unfriended—mother, thou wilt be
    Alone at morn and eve.

And through the long, long day,
Thou'lt sit with breaking heart above thy task,
Earning thy daily bread, while others bask
    In fortune's sunny ray.

For on thy heart will press
A thousand memories of thy buried child,
And thou wilt pour thy weepings long and wild,
    In utter loneliness.

And, in the time of sleep,
Thou'lt turn to kiss me as thou oft hast done,
But memory will whisper "she is gone,"
    And thou wilt wake and weep.

Before my father died,
We dwelt beneath our own bright stately halls,
Round which blue streams and silver fountain-falls
    Were seen to glide.

There, on the evening breeze
In summer-time, no harsher sound was heard
Than the low flutter of some singing bird,
    Startled among the trees.

And there, beside our hearth,
Thou'st often knelt and offered up to God
My infant spirit, pure as snow untrod,
    And free from taint of earth.

But now, how changed thy lot!
Strangers are dwelling in our once bright home,
While thou art pent within this close dark room,
    Unaided and forgot.

I have been like a spell,
Binding thee unto earth, but death hath pressed
His cold and heavy hand upon my breast—
Mother, I go—farewell!

Slowly her arms unwound their wreathing clasp
Around her mother's neck, and her fair head
Fell heavy back, while a low lengthened gasp
Stirred her cold marble bosom—she was dead.
Silent that mother gazed, the mighty flood
Of grief within her breast she strove to hide,
For it seemed sin to weep, while thus she stood
Above the holy dead, the sanctified.

It was no time to mourn, for she had yet
A bitter mournful duty to fulfil,
To press the eyelids o'er the blue orbs set,
To close the sweet lips smiling on her still;
She laid the ringlets round the lifeless face,
And wrapped the loose shroud round the slender form,
That lay in mute and melancholy grace
As if spell-bound in slumber soft and warm.

THE DYING GIRL.

And when the stars of night began to wane,
And the warm sun had chased away the gloom,
Strange forms were seen around the lattice-pane,
That looked into that dim and dreary room;
And as they crossed the threshold of the door,
They found her drooping by her daughter's bed,
Her raven tresses streaming o'er the floor
And her dark glassy eye fixed on the dead.

O! 'twas indeed a sadly touching sight,
For her white hand lay pressed upon her heart,
As if to quell within the spirit's might,
And her cold purple lips were half apart:
They raised her from the spot where she had knelt
In the meek attitude of holy prayer,
And with the nicest touch her bosom felt,
Seeking for life and warmth—but death was there!

THE NEGLECTED HARP.

O! why art thou left, thou lone harp, here,
   With none to awake thy slumbers,
Save the minstrel wind as it lingers near
   To call forth thy plaintive numbers!

O sadly sweet is the wild, wild strain,
   That over thy light chords lingers;
For ne'er will those light chords breathe again
   To the touch of a mortal's fingers.

The hand, that once caused thy chords to thrill,
   A lovelier harp may awaken,
But the spirit of music will haunt thee still,
   Although by that hand forsaken.

THE NEGLECTED HARP.

And she, who around thee roses flung,
  May wreathe them in brighter bowers;
Yet sweetness around thy chords hath clung,
  And perfume around thy flowers.

I pity thee for each altered tone,
  That once gushed forth in gladness,
For now, like a charmless thing, thou'rt thrown
  To breathe out those tones in sadness

I pity thee for each music-sigh,
  Lost on the winds of heaven,
For the wasted flow of thy melody,
  To the wandering zephyrs given.

Ah! thus it is with fond woman's heart,
  When love comes o'er it stealing;
To each thrilling touch its chords impart
  The music of every feeling.

THE NEGLECTED HARP.

Sorrow may o'er her spirit come,
   Her brightest dreams dispelling,
Yet still, like a flower, her heart will bloom
   If love in its depths is swelling.

And e'en should the spell, round her warm heart wove,
   Be broke by the being that bound it,
Still memory will sweep o'er its chords of love,
   And sweetness will linger around it.

I mourn, thou harp, for no touch may bring
   Back thy sweet tones departed,
Yet more do I mourn, thou wailing thing,
   O'er the lost and the broken-hearted.

THE STARS.

Love ye the blossoms, whose rosy tints, blending,
　Glow bright as the hues of our own sunny sky,
When their young buds unfolding, with fresh dew-drops bending,
　Fling forth their rich breathings on each passer-by?

Love ye the winds round our fragrant paths stealing,
　The soft winds that sigh through the long summer hours,
As they wake in the bosom, some long-slumbered feeling,
　Then nestle away to the hearts of the flowers?

Love ye those dreams, that so often steal o'er us,
　When no sigh in the breast its tranquillity mars,
When visions of beauty dance gayly before us?
　Yet love ye not better the stars, the bright stars?

THE STARS.

Give, give me the orbs, that in brightness are beaming,
    When twilight her soft silver drapery lowers;
For, when stars are shining, who, who would be dreaming,
    Or listening to wild winds, or gazing on flowers!

'Tis not that the blossoms have failed to awaken
    Within my young bosom sweet feelings of love,
That so oft by my glance their soft hues are forsaken
    For those bright things, that glitter in radiance above.

For I know that our hearts would be dreary without them,
    Those sweet buds of hope 'mid the thorns of despair,
And may all the beauty and perfume about them
    Still brighten the green earth and sweeten the air.

Yet still I have thought, when misfortunes o'ertook us,
    And those we had cherished have laughed at our doom,
That the flowers were emblems of those who forsook us,
    For they smile in the sunshine, but shrink from the gloom.

But the stars, the soft stars, when they glitter above us,
   I gaze on their beams with a feeling divine,
For, as true friends in sorrow more tenderly love us,
   The darker the hour the brighter they shine.

Give, give me the hour when the day-god reposing
   Has sunk in the far west behind his gold bars,
For when shades gather round us and flowers are closing,
   They burst forth in glory, the stars, the bright stars!

THE DEW-DROP

I AM a sparkling drop of dew,
   Just wept from yon silver star,
But drops of dew have very few
   To care for what they are ;
For little ye dream, who dwell below,
   Of all I've wandered through ;
Ye only know I sparkle so,
   Because I'm a drop of dew.

I flashed at first with waves, that whirl
   O'er the blue, blue, tossing sea ;
Where eddies curl o'er beds of pearl
   I wandered wild and free,

'Till I chanced to spy an elfin king,
    And I danced before his view,
When the merry thing, with his glittering wing,
    Whisked off the drop of dew.

The evening air with sweets was fraught,
    And away we flitted far,
When, quick as thought, I was upward caught,
    To yon lovely vesper star;
And I'm very sure a gentle charm
    That bright thing round me threw,
For an angel form, in her bosom warm,
    Enfolded the drop of dew.

But I slept not long in yon starry bower,
    In the bosom of my love,
For, in a shower, to this primrose flower,
    She sent me from above;
And soon its moonlight leaves will close,
    But they hide me not from view,
For the wind, that flows o'er the young primrose,
    Will kiss off the drop of dew

THE SLEEPING MAIDEN.

Bright as the spell of loveliness
   Cast round thee, maiden, here,
Are the sweet dreams, that angels now
   Are whispering in thy ear;
Yes, very bright and very sweet
   Those dreamings all must be,
Or else they would not flit around
   A creature fair as thee.

O! beautiful indeed thou art
   As some pure spirit blest,
With thy gold tresses gleaming soft,
   Like sunbeams, o'er thy breast;

THE SLEEPING MAIDEN.

And thy rose-tinted cheek, now bright
    As the first blush of day,
Now faint as if a zephyr's sigh
    Could brush its bloom away—

And thy bright glances, gathered all
    Beneath each snowy lid,
That, silken-fringed, rests lightly o'er
    The beauty they have hid,
Giving unto thy lovely face
    A pensive twilight ray,
Like that which tints the summer sky
    When sunbeams fade away.

Sweetly from thy deep dreaming breast,
    Thy thoughts are gushing now,
Like perfume up to Him, who threw
    Such beauty o'er thy brow;
Thoughts, lovelier, holier far than those
    That haunt thy waking hours,
And fresh as dew-drops on the leaves
    Of odor-breathing flowers.

I would that thou shouldst ever be
    Thus free from weary care,
That thy young brow its holy calm
    On earth may ever wear.
But, as such perfect happiness
    To mortals is not given,
I'd have thee dream thy life away,
    And only wake in heaven.

MY OWN NATIVE LAND.

O! talk not to me of fair Italy's sky.
Of the soft perfumed gales, that through Araby sigh;
I know there is not on this wide-spreading earth
A land bright and free as this land of my birth;
We have our mild zephyrs and bright sunny beams,
Our fruits and our flowers, fair valleys and streams;
Thy rocks and thy mountains are lofty and grand,
And brave are thy children, my own native land.

If cowards and tyrants e'er seek to enchain,
And bring to the dust our proud spirits again;
Thy sons, still united, will rally for thee,
And die, as they've lived, the exalted and free!

O! had I the strength of my heart in my hand,
I'd fight for thy freedom, my own native land;
Amid thy oppressors undaunted I'd fly,
And fling forth our banner in triumph on high.

TO MRS. S. J. P——.

LADY, the last lay of thy muse's lyre
   Hath stirred the deep tides of my youthful soul;
The strain hath lulled to rest each wild desire,
   And soothed my feelings with its soft control;
Canst thou to me thy magic power impart,
The power to please the ear, and melt the heart?

'Tis with an untaught hand I sweep the chords,
   Which yield to thee their softest, sweetest tone;
The only melody my touch affords
   Is wild and mournful as a wind-harp's moan;
But lyre and song are both too weak to tell
The thoughts, that in my throbbing bosom swell.

But thou hast bid me learn to quell and hush
    My thrilling feelings in my bosom deep,
To bid them all, when forth they fain would rush,
    Back to their cells, in silence there to sleep;
Ah! I have long since learned that bitter task,
To hide my feelings 'neath a different mask.

I know thee not, and yet our spirits seem
    Together linked by sympathy and love,
And, like the mingled waters of a stream,
    Our thoughts and fancies all united rove;
Our hands were never clasped, our lips ne'er met,
Yet still thine image on my mind is set.

I think of thee, sweet lady, as of one
    Too pure to mix with others, like some star
Shining in pensive beauty all alone,
    Kindred with those around, yet brighter far;
O! if I have one wish, it is to be
Such as my glowing fancy pictures thee!

THE DYING MOTHER.

On breezy pinion, mournful eve came singing
   Over the silent hills, and to the glades
And violet-beds a stream of odors bringing,
   And waking music in the forest shades;
For 'twas the time, when the lone cotter, wending
   His silent way along the footpaths dim,
Sought his loved home, where gentle voices blending
   Sent up the music of an evening hymn.

A lovely length of moonlit waters lightly
   Broke into sudden brightness on the strand,
While through the sky's soft fleecy fret-work brightly
   The stars looked out upon the stilly land;

But sadly 'neath them gleamed two lovely faces,
  (O! fearful things and sad the stars do see,)
For they were strangers roaming through strange places—
  A mother with her boy beside her knee.

Her only shelter was the blue-arched heaven,
  As to her child's she bent her earnest face,
For well she knew another whispering even
  Would find her form a thing for Death's embrace;
And, as she saw the quivering tear-drop springing
  Into his eyes, and heard him ask for bread,
Swift thoughts, like lightning, through her brain went winging,
  And thus she poured them o'er his fair young head.

Boy! I would fain return thy fond caresses,
  But I must put thee from my heart away
    On the cold earth to lay;
And though upon thee Hunger harshly presses,
  Planting within thee deep its gnawing fangs,
    I cannot stay thy pangs.

THE DYING MOTHER.

For I have wandered till I'm worn and weary,
Seeking a shelter for thy little head,
   Or a spare crust of bread;
But have found none, and now, heart-sick and dreary,
I lay me down beneath the quiet sky
   To bless thee, boy, and die.

It is, alas! a mournful thing to leave thee
In this cold world to thy young thoughts alone;
   For O! when I am gone,
No smiling mother will at eve receive thee,
Bending o'er thy hushed lip and folded eye—
   Alas! that I must die!

But thou wilt think upon the prayer I taught thee,
When life with us flowed smoothly as a song
   Our native hills among,
And how at noontide 1 have often brought thee,
In thy young beauty, to thy father's side,
   With all a mother's pride.

And when for rest thou seek'st the rich man's dwelling,
Should he from his bright mansion bid thee flee,
    Speaking harsh things to thee,
Let not thy heart with dark despair be swelling,
For soft to thee will be the velvet sod,
    If thou wilt trust in God.

And each pale lily, o'er the waters stooping,
From 'ts pure alabaster vase will shed
    A gleam about thy head;
And the rich berries in red clusters drooping
From many a bended bough in this dark wood,
    Will be thy fragrant food.

For thou must wander by each low-voiced river,
And school thy timid heart to be alone
    When the night-winds make moan;
And, when the forest leaves above thee shiver,
To calmly lay thee 'neath their solemn shade,
    And not to be afraid.

THE DYING MOTHER.

For He, who in his glory dwells above thee,
Who tempereth the wind to the shorn lamb,
    With a deep Sabbath calm
Will fill thy heart, and in his mercy love thee,
And on thy weakness bend a pitying eye,
    And in thy need draw nigh.

And now, farewell! the early morn will wake thee
Unto a fearful sight—thy mother, child,
    Dead in a forest-wild;
And sudden sorrow, like a storm will shake thee,
But God will still the tempest in thy breast—
    A blessing on thee rest!

SWEET BE THY DREAMS

Sweet be thy dreams when balmy sleep
  Her soothing influence round thee throws!
What if my faded eyes should weep?
  Thine will be folded to repose.
I know thou wilt not dream of me;
  Some lovelier one will haunt thy rest;
I care not what those dreams may be,
  So they are sweet and thou art blessed.

Bright be thy hopes! why should one cloud
  Of sorrow dim thy radiant eye?
Go! mingle with the gay and proud,
  And learn to smile, though I may sigh;

Go ! climb the loftiest steep of fame,
  And wreathe a laurel round thy brow ;
And when thou'st won a glorious name,
  Low at the shrine of beauty bow.

Light be thy heart! why shouldst thou keep
  Sadness within its secret cells ?
Let not thine eye one tear-drop weep,
  Unless that tear of rapture tells ;
Go ! shed on all thy brightest beams ;
  I would, but must not, bid thee stay ;
Sweet vision of my sweetest dreams !
  In dream-like beauty pass away.

THE VIOLET'S SONG TO THE LOST FAIRY.

Come to me, fairy queen,
   Stars o'er thee, lightly
Floating in dazzling sheen,
   Glimmer out brightly;
Moonbeams are glittering
   On each pure blossom—
Fold up thy weary wing,
   Come to my bosom.

Sleep, like a dewy cloud,
   On thy brow presses;
Round thy form, like a shroud,
   Droop thy fair tresses:

Heavy thine eyelids close
    O'er thy glance shaded;
I'll give thee soft repose,
    Thou lost and faded.

Each lily's pearly cup
    Sheds out pale gleamings;
Roses are folded up
    To their sweet dreamings;
Hark! how the night-winds pass,
    Mournfully sighing,
Through the down-trailing grass—
    Where art thou flying?

Where the young willow-boughs
    Greenly are waving,
Where the blue streamlet flows
    Sunny banks laving,
There sit thy fairy few,
    Their glances veiling
'Neath tears that fall like dew,
    Thy loss bewailing.

I've oped my azure bell
  Wide to receive thee,
Where if thou'lt ever dwell
  None may deceive thee;
I'll breathe my faint perfume
  On thy lip only—
Love thee through joy and gloom,
  Thou fair and lonely.

TO A SEA-SHELL.

SHELL of the bright sea-waves!
What is it, that we hear in thy sad moan?
Is this unceasing music all thine own?
    Lute of the ocean-caves!

O does some spirit dwell
In tne deep windings of thy chambers dim,
Breathing forever, in its mournful hymn,
    Of ocean's anthem swell?

Wert thou a murmurer long
In crystal palaces beneath the seas,
Ere from the blue sky thou hadst heard the breeze
    Pour its full tide of song?

TO A SEA-SHELL.

    Another thing with thee—
Are there not gorgeous cities in the deep,
Buried with flashing gems that brightly sleep,
    Hid by the mighty sea?

    And say, O lone sea-shell!
Are there not costly things and sweet perfumes
Scattered in waste o'er that sea-gulf of tombs?
    Hush thy low moan and tell.

    But yet, and more than all—
Has not each foaming wave in fury tossed
O'er earth's most beautiful, the brave, the lost,
    Like a dark funeral pall?

    'Tis vain—thou answerest not!
Thou hast no voice to whisper of the dead;
'Tis ours alone, with sighs like odors shed,
    To hold them unforgot!

TO A SEA-SHELL.

Thine is as sad a strain
As if the spirit in thy hidden cell
Pined to be with the many things, that dwell
In the wild restless main.

And yet there is no sound
Upon the waters, whispered by the waves,
But seemeth like a wail from many graves,
Thrilling the air around.

The earth, O moaning shell!
The earth hath melodies more sweet than these- -
The music gush of rills, the hum of bees
Heard in each blossom's bell.

Are not these tones of earth,
The rustling forest, with its shivering leaves,
Sweeter than sounds that e'en in moonlit eves
Upon the seas have birth?

TO A SEA-SHELL.

Alas! thou still wilt moan—
Thou'rt like the heart that wastes itself in sighs
E'en when amid bewildering melodies,
If parted from its own.

TO MRS. L——.

LADY, if hope's bright ray
   Deceive thee with its beam,
If life's joys melt away
   Like love's first witching dream,
If all earth's tender ties
   Have from thy heart been riven,
Look up beyond the skies—
   To tenderer ties in heaven.

If all the buds of earth,
   That promised early bloom,
Have perished in their birth
   Like beauty in the tomb,

If love hath seared thy heart,
A glorious hope is given,
Which soothes affliction's smart—
There's purer love in heaven.

LINES WRITTEN WHILE GAZING ON A BEAUTIFUL LITTLE GIRL GATHERING FLOWERS.

I LOVE to gaze on thy face, fair child,
    For thou seemest too bright for earth;
There's a music-tone in thy laughter wild,
    As it breaks from thy heart of mirth.

Affection speaks in thy soft blue eye,
    As its restless glances rove,
Thy voice of glee comes ringing by—
    Alas! for thy heart of love.

Ah! many a bright and airy dream
  Hath over thy spirit passed,
Like sunshine o'er a laughing stream,
  Too beautiful to last.

I sigh to think of the transient joy
  That illumines thy gladsome youth,
Of the guile and deceit that will soon destroy
  Thy feelings of warmth and truth.

Thou'rt plucking away from their slender stems
  The rose and the lily fair,
Their bright leaves glittering with dewy gems,
  To wreathe in thy golden hair.

And now thou'rt crowned, like a fairy queen,
  With flowerets of many a hue,
Thy brow 'neath their velvet leaves is seen
  Like a snow-flake shining through.

The rose, with its sofest, richest dyes,
    Scarce rivals thy downy cheek,
Thy dewy lip with each blossom vies,
    And thine eyes with the violets meek.

Thou seemest to me but a brighter flower
    Just budding with beauty rife,
And deeming the world all a fairy bower—
    Ah! this is thy dream of life.

But childhood will flee, and with riper years
    Thy thoughts will be borne away;
With a bosom thrilling with hopes and fears,
    Thou wilt move mid the fair and gay.

The feelings that now in thy bosom sleep,
    Will burst from their dreamy thrall;
Alas! that love like a blight should creep,
    And wither those feelings all.

Ah! then thou wilt taste of the cup of wo
   If thy pure deep love be spurned,
For hearts, that like thine with affection glow,
   Have seldom their love returned.

Alas! that one care of earth should mar
   The beauty that seems divine—
That thine eye, like a softly gleaming star,
   Should e'er through a tear-drop shine.

THE DREAMERS.

COUNTLESS as the stars, whose numbers
   Mock us where their brightness glows,
Are the dreams that haunt our slumbers
   When we're gathered to repose;
And, as each soft starry peeper
   Bursts forth in its own bright beam,
So it is with every sleeper—
   Each one hath a separate dream.

Mother, on thy couch reclining
   With thy pale cheek wet with tears,
Sleep around thy heart is twining
   Buried hopes of former years;

Dream'st thou of each faded blossom,
    Folded once upon thy breast?
Mourn not, for within His bosom
    They have found a safer rest.

Maiden, whose warm cheek is glowing
    With the spirit of thy dreams,
Each wild bud of fancy blowing
    To thy mind as real seems;
Honeyed words by sweet lips spoken
    Round thee have their witchery cast;
May the charm remain unbroken
    When thy nightly dream is past.

Child of gladness, thou art sinking
    To thy sweet rest soft and deep,
For the thirsty flowers are drinking
    Every tear the bright stars weep;
As the silvery light of even
    Gathers round the parting day,
So do gentle dreams of heaven
    Flit about thee—dream away.

THE DREAMERS.

Weary warrior, lately grasping
    In thy hand the flashing blade,
In sweet dreams thou'rt fondly clasping
    Lovely forms now lowly laid;
Rosy lips thine own are pressing,
    Fairy children round thee play,
But with every transient blessing
    Melts that soothing dream away.

Lonely captive, sleep is flinging
    Round thee many a witching spell;
Low sweet tones are round thee ringing,
    Tones, that lately breathed farewell;
Clanking chains thy limbs encumber—
    Hush! ye wild winds, peaceful be—
Break not yet the captive's slumber—
    Rosy sleep hath set him free!

Mortals, when those dreams are over,
    Praise His name, who round us flings
Visions bright, and bids us hover
    'Neath the shadow of His wings.

Soon that deep sleep will o'ertake us,
Sleep, that passeth not away,
Till the last trump shall awake us
To one bright eternal day.

MAY.

O, THIS is the beautiful month of May,
    The season of birds and of flowers ;
The young and the lovely are out and away,
Mid the up-springing grass and the blossoms, at play ;
And many a heart will be happy to-day,
    In this beautiful region of ours.

Sweet April, the frail, the capriciously bright,
    Hath passed like the lovely away,
Yet we mourn not her absence, for swift at her flight
Sprang forth her young sister, an angel of light,
And fair as a sunbeam that dazzles the sight,
    Is beautiful, beautiful May.

What scenes of delight, what sweet visions she brings
  Of freshness, of gladness, and mirth,
Of fair sunny glades where the buttercup springs,
Of cool gushing fountains, of rose-tinted wings,
Of birds, bees, and blossoms, all beautiful things,
  Whose brightness rejoices the earth.

How fair is the landscape! o'er hill-top and glade,
  What swift-varying colors are rolled—
The shadow now sunshine, the sunshine now shade;
Their light-shifting hues for the green earth have made
A garment resplendent with dew-gems o'erlaid—
  A light-woven tissue of gold!

O yes! lovely May, the enchantingly fair,
  Is here with her beams and her flowers;
Their rainbow-like garments the blossoms now wear,
And all in their health-giving odors may share,
For the breath of their sweetness is out on the air,
  Those children of sunbeams and showers.

MAY.

The fragrant magnolia in loveliness dressed,
    The lilac's more delicate hue,
The violet half opening its azure-hued vest,
Just kissed by a sunbeam, its innocent guest,
The light floating cloudlets like spirits at rest,
    All pictured in motionless blue—

These brighten the landscape, and softly unroll
    Their splendors by land and by sea;
They steal o'er the heart with a magic control,
That lightens the bosom and freshens the soul—
O! this is the charm that enhances the whole,
    And makes them so lovely to me.

How sweet, when the month's in the flush of its prime,
    To hear, as we wander alone,
Some bird's sudden song from the sweet-scented lime,
And catch the low gush of its exquisite chime,
And set it to music and turn it to rhyme,
    With a spirit as light as its own.

And sweet to recline 'neath the emerald-robed trees,
    Where fairy-like footsteps have trod,
With the lull of the waters, the hum of the bees,
Melting into the spirit delicious degrees
Of exquisite softness! in moments like these,
    I have walked with the angels of God.

Sweet season of love, when the fairy-queen trips
    At eve through the stsr-lighted grove—
What vows are now breathed where the honey-bee sips!
What cheeks, whose bright beauties the roses eclipse,
Are crimsoned with blushes! what rose-tinted lips
    Are moist with the kisses of love!

Yet, loveliest of months! with the praises I sing,
    Thy glories are passing away
With the dew from the blossom, the bird on the wing,
Yet round thee a garland poetic I fling,
Sweet sister of April! young child of the Spring!
    O beautiful, beautiful May!

PULPIT ELOQUENCE.

THE day was declining—the breeze in its glee
Had left the fair blossoms to sing on the sea,
As the sun in its gorgeousness, radiant and still,
Dropped down like a gem from the brow of the hill;
One tremulous star, in the glory of June,
Came out with a smile and sat down by the moon,
As she graced her blue throne with the pride of a queen,
The smiles of her loveliness gladdening the scene.

The scene was enchanting! in distance away
Rolled the foam-crested waves of the Chesapeake bay,
While bathed in the moonlight the village was seen,
With the church in the distance that stood on the green,

The soft-sloping meadows lay brightly unrolled
With their mantles of verdure and blossoms of gold,
And the earth in her beauty, forgetting to grieve,
Lay asleep in her bloom on the bosom of eve.

A light-hearted child I had wandered away
From the spot where my footsteps had gambolled all day,
And free as a bird's was the song of my soul,
As I heard the wild waters exultingly roll,
While, lightening my heart as I sported along
With bursts of low laughter and snatches of song,
I struck in the pathway half-worn o'er the sod
By the feet that went up to the worship of God.

As I traced its green windings, a murmur of prayer
With the hymn of the worshippers rose on the air.
And, drawn by the links of its sweetness along,
I stood unobserved in the midst of the throng;
For awhile my young spirit still wandered about
With the birds, and the winds, that were singing without,
But birds, waves, and zephyrs were quickly forgot
In one angel-like being that brightened the spot.

In stature majestic, apart from the throng
He stood in his beauty, the theme of my song!
His cheek pale with fervor—the blue orbs above
Lit up with the splendors of youth and of love;
Yet the heart-glowing raptures, that beamed from those eyes
Seemed saddened by sorrows, and chastened by sighs,
As if the young heart in its bloom had grown cold
With its loves unrequited, its sorrows untold.

Such language as his I may never recall;
But his theme was salvation—salvation to all;
And the souls of a thousand in ecstasy hung
On the manna-like sweetness that dropped from his tongue;
Not alone on the ear his wild eloquence stole;
Enforced by each gesture it sank to the soul,
Till it seemed that an angel had brightened the sod
And brought to each bosom a message from God.

He spoke of the Saviour—what pictures he drew!
The scene of His sufferings rose clear on my view—
The cross—the rude cross where he suffered and died,
The gush of bright crimson that flowed from His side,

The cup of his sorrows, the wormwood and gall,
The darkness that mantled the earth as a pall,
The garland of thorns, and the demon-like crews,
Who knelt as they scoffed Him—" Hail, King of the Jews !"

He spake, and it seemed that his statue-like form
Expanded and glowed as his spirit grew warm—
His tone so impassioned, so melting his air,
As touched with compassion, he ended in prayer,
His hands clasped above him, his blue orbs upthrown,
Still pleading for sins that were never his own,
While that mouth, where such sweetness ineffable clung,
Still spoke, though expression had died on his tongue.

O God ! what emotions the speaker awoke !
A mortal he seemed—yet a deity spoke ;
A man—yet so far from humanity riven !
On earth—yet so closely connected with heaven !
How oft in my fancy I've pictured him there,
As he stood in that triumph of passion and prayer,
With his eyes closed in rapture—their transient eclipse
Made bright by the smiles that illumined his lips.

PULPIT ELOQUENCE.

There's a charm in delivery, a magical art,
That thrills, like a kiss, from the lip to the heart;
'Tis the glance—the expression—the well-chosen word,
By whose magic the depths of the spirit are stirred,
The smile—the mute gesture—the soul-startling pause,
The eye's sweet expression—that melts while it awes,
The lip's soft persuasion—its musical tone—
O such was the charm of that eloquent one!

The time is long past, yet how clearly defined
That bay, church, and village, float up on my mind!
I see amid azure the moon in her pride,
With the sweet little trembler, that sat by her side,
I hear the blue waves, as she wanders along,
Leap up in their gladness and sing her a song,
And I tread in the pathway half-worn o'er the sod
By the feet that went up to the worship of God.

The time is long past, yet what visions I see!
The past, the dim past, is the present to me;
I am standing once more mid that heart-stricken throng
A vision floats up—'tis the theme of my song—

All glorious and bright as a spirit of air,
The light like a halo encircling his hair—
As I catch the same accents of sweetness and love,
He whispers of Jesus—and points us above.

How sweet to my heart is the picture I've traced!
Its chain of bright fancies seemed almost effaced,
Till memory, the fond one, that sits in the soul,
Took up the frail links, and connected the whole:
As the dew to the blossom, the bud to the bee,
As the scent to the rose, are those memories to me;
Round the chords of my heart they have tremblingly clung,
And the echo it gives is the song I have sung.

THE LAST INTERVIEW.

HERE, in this lonely bower where first I won thee,
   I come, beloved, beneath the moon's pale ray,
To gaze, once more, through struggling tears upon thee,
   And then to bear my broken heart away;
I dare not linger near thee as a brother,
   I feel my burning heart would still be thine;
How could I hope my passionate thoughts to smother,
While yielding all the sweetness to another,
      That should be mine!

But fate hath willed it; the decree is spoken;
   Now life may lengthen out its weary chain;
For, reft of thee, its loveliest links are broken;
   May we but clasp them all in Heaven again!

THE LAST INTERVIEW.

Yes, thou wilt there be mine; in yon blue heaven
   There are sweet meetings of the pure and fond;
O! joys unspeakable to such are given,
When the sweet ties of love, that here are riven,
      Unite beyond.

A glorious charm from Heaven thou dost inherit;
   The gift of angels unto thee belongs;
Then breathe thy love in music, that thy spirit
   May whisper to me through thine own sweet songs;
And though my coming life may soon resemble
   The desert-spots through which my steps will flee,
Though round thee then wild worshippers assemble,
My heart will triumph if thine own but tremble
      Still true to me.

Yet, not when on our bower the light reposes
   In golden glory, wilt thou sigh for me,
Not when the young bee seeks the crimson roses
   And the far sunbeams tremble o'er the sea;

But when at eve the tender heart grows fonder,
  And the full soul with pensive love is fraught,
Then with wet lids o'er these sweet paths thou'lt wander,
And, thrilled with love, upon my memory ponder
  With tender thought.

And when at times thy bird-like voice entrances
  The listening throng with some enchanting lay,
If I am near thee, let thy heavenly glances
  One gentle message to my heart convey;
I ask but this—a happier one has taken
  From my lone life the charm that made it dear;
I ask but this, and promise thee unshaken
To meet that look of love—but O! 'twill awaken
  Such raptures here!

And now farewell! farewell! I dare not lengthen
  These sweet sad moments out; to gaze on thee
Is bliss indeed, yet it but serves to strengthen
  The love that now amounts to agony;

THE LAST INTERVIEW.

This is our last farewell, our last fond meeting;
   The world is wide, and we must dwell apart;
My spirit gives thee, now, its last wild greeting,
With lip to lip, while pulse to pulse is beating,
   And heart to heart.

Farewell! farewell! our dream of bliss is over,
   All, save the memory of our plighted love;
I now must yield thee to thy happier lover,
   Yet, O remember, thou art mine above!
'Tis a sweet thought, and, when by distance parted,
   'Twill lie upon our hearts a holy spell;
But the sad tears beneath thy lids have started,
And I—alas! we both are broken-hearted—
   Dearest, farewell!

WHEN SOFT STARS.

When soft stars are peeping
   Through the pure azure sky,
And southern gales sweeping
   Their warm breathings by
Like sweet music pealing
   Far o'er the blue sea
There come o'er me stealing
   Sweet memories of thee.

The bright rose when faded
   Flings forth o'er its tomb
Its velvet leaves laded
   With silent perfume:

Thus round me will hover
In grief, or in glee,
Till Life's dream be over,
Sweet memories of thee.

As a sweet lute, that lingers
In silence alone,
Unswept by light fingers,
Scarce murmurs a tone,
My young heart resembled
That lute light and free,
Till o'er its chords trembled,
Those memories of thee.

O! HAD WE ONLY MET.

O! HAD we only met
    When life and hope were new,
When love, unmingled with regret,
    Lay on our hearts like dew,
I had not heaved a sigh
    When, wrapt in that sweet trance,
I raised my *own* and met thine eye,
    Returning glance for glance.

O! do not prize me less
    For yielding to the power,
The soft delicious dreaminess,
    That filled that twilight hour;

O! HAD WE ONLY MET.

I thought its spells were thine,
    Around my spirit wove,
And half forgot it was not mine
    To give thee love for love.

Love! Did I call it love?
    It will not bear the name!
A softer thought our bosoms move,
    A tenderer, milder flame;
I feel it in the tone
    That thrilled thy low reply,
As thy warm lip, beside my own,
    Responded sigh for sigh.

I love thee not, but O!
    If we had met in youth,
When first we dreamed of passion's glow,
    Its fervor and its truth,
Perhaps it had been mine,
    With whispers soft and low,
To place my little hand in thine,
    And murmur vow for vow.

O! HAD WE ONLY MET.

Dear one! for dear thou art,
    Thou know'st it is not mine
To lift the veil from this deep heart
    Nor yet to gaze in thine;
But O! were I to speak
    Of all I hope and fear,
Even thou wouldst scarcely deem it weak,
    To give me tear for tear.

TO AMANDA

SWEET lady, wilt thou think of me
  When Music's tones are round thee thrilling
With a soft gushing melody,
  Thy gentle heart with rapture filling?
O let my voice, like that loved strain,
  Touch in thy heart the chords of feeling,
Like long-hushed music, breathed again
  By zephyrs, o'er a wind-harp stealing.

Sweet lady, wilt thou think of me
  When Friendship's flowers are round thee wreathing,
And Love's delicious flattery
  Within thy ear is softly breathing?

TO AMANDA.

O let my friendship in the wreath,
   Though but a bud amid the flowers,
Its sweetest fragrance round thee breathe—
   'Twill serve to soothe thy weary hours.

Sweet lady, wilt thou think of me?
   Ah, should we e'er by fate be parted,
Wilt thou embalm my memory,
   The memory of the loving-hearted!
O let our spirits then unite,
   Each silent eve, in sweet communion!
Our thoughts will mingle in their flight,
   And heaven will bless the secret union.

MUSIC.

O'er the bright moonlit sea
   Let music swell;
Breathe round me melody
   Where'er I dwell.

If on the ocean deep
   Lonely I roam,
Let music round me sweep—
   Music of home.

As the tones mingling float
   With the waves play,
Soothing will be each note,
   Melting away.

When mid the gladsome throng,
  Joyous I feel,
Let a rich tide of song
  Soft round me steal.

Or should my pensive heart
  Feel sad and lone,
There's naught can heal each smart
  Like music's tone

When I am touched by death—
  On some loved breast,
Listening to music's breath,
  Lull me to rest.

And when I'm borne along
  To my last sleep,
Break forth in mournful song
  Mellow and deep.

O'er the bright moonlit sea
Let music swell,
Breathe round me melody
Where'er I dwell.

THE BRIDE.

A FRINGE of dewy leaves,
   Along the branches droop,
That overhang the cottage-eaves,
   Where stand a bridal group;
In fair and laughing bands
   The maidens, far and wide,
Have brought fresh roses in their hands,
   To crown the fair young bride.

Before the man of prayer,
   They slowly gather round,
As silent as the floating air,
   That floats without a sound,

THE BRIDE.

As, with a downcast brow,
    Close to her lover's side,
Comes forth in raiment white as snow
    The young and timid bride

How beautiful she seems,
    As o'er her soft brown hair
The sunset flings its golden gleams,
    And forms a halo there,
While o'er her features play
    The tnoughts she cannot hide,
Whose soft expression seems to say,
    I am thy happy bride.

No cold vain look is there,
    But all is soft and meek;
Upon her virgin forehead fair,
    And o'er her dimpled cheek,
A something soft and warm,
    That round her seems to glide,
Involves as with a heavenly charm
    The young and spotless bride.

THE BRIDE

There's a whispered vow of love,
    As side by side they stand,
And the drawing of a snow-white glove
    From a little trembling hand,
And the glitter of a ring,
    And a tear that none may chide—
These, these have changed that girlish thing,
    And she is now a bride.

No shadow dims her brow—
    She feels without a fear
The trusting love that all may know,
    Who wed in their own sphere: .
And he, who clasps her now,
    All flushed with love and pride,
Has breathed to her his holiest vow,
    And takes her for his bride.

Sweet bride! he'll ne'er forget,
    When 'neath thy father's cot
He met thee like a violet,
    Within a shady spot.

THE BRIDE.

Through all the balmy air,
   And the breathing world beside,
There's naught to him so soft and fair
   As thou, his blessed bride.

Sweet tie! that links as one
   Two spirits fond and true—
What, what is all that time has done,
   Or all that time can do!
Recorded vows of love,
   In heaven fore'er abide,
And none shall part, save One above,
   The bridegroom and the bride.

THE MOURNFUL HEART.

My heart is like a lonely bird,
    That sadly sings,
Brooding upon its nest unheard,
    With folded wings.

For of my thoughts the sweetest part
    Lie all untold,
And treasured in this mournful heart
    Like precious gold.

The fever-dreams that haunt my soul
    Are deep and strong;
For through its deep recesses roll
    Such floods of song.

I strive to calm, to lull to rest,
    Each mournful strain,
To lay the phantom in my breast—
    But ah! 'tis vain.

The glory of the silent skies,
    Each kindling star,
The young leaves stirred with melodies,
    My quiet mar.

O! in my soul too wild and strong
    This gift hath grown,
Bright spirit of immortal song!
    Take back thine own.

I know no sorrows round me cling,
    My years are few;
And yet my heart's the saddest thing
    I ever knew.

THE MOURNFUL HEART.

For in my thoughts the world doth share
But little part;
A mournful thing it is to bear
A mournful heart.

THE PARTED YEAR.

The parted year hath passed away
  Unto that dreamy land,
Where ages upon ages sleep,
  A mighty, slumbering band,
And, like a blood-stained conqueror
  Grown weary of renown,
Hath yielded to the new-born year
  His sceptre and his crown.

Hushed now should be each tone of glee,
  Unquaffed the sparkling wine,
While Love and Grief bow hand in hand
  At Memory's sacred shrine ;

E'en haughty Pride should humbly bend
　Down from his lofty steep,
And from the banquet laughing Mirth
　Should turn aside and weep.

Unwearied Thought, with solemn brow,
　Droops o'er the heart's deep urn,
And traces on its glowing page,
　The past will ne'er return.
While Fancy from her starry height
　Returns with mournful eye,
And, folding up her rainbow wing,
　Stands meekly pensive by.

Hark! the low winds are sighing now
　O'er the departed year,
And gathering in dim autumn leaves,
　To strew upon His bier,
While the tall trees stand leafless round,
　Unstirred by summer's breath,
Like mourners reft of every hope
　Above the couch of death.

But now the sepulchre of years
    Hath closed its portals o'er
The form of the departed year
    In silence as before;
And the New-Year with stately **tread**
    Steals slowly o'er the earth,
Robed in the garments of his state,
    A monarch from his birth.

Could we but lift the mildewed veil
    O'er buried ages cast,
And bring to light the darkened things
    That slumber with the past,
Sad mysteries, undreamed of now,
    One glance would then unfold,
And many other mournful things,
    Too mournful to be told.

The cold, the dead, the beautiful,
    E'en now they silent pass
Like floating shadows, one by one,
    O'er memory's faithful glass;

And Hope and Love start fondly up
    To greet them as of yore,
But something whispers unto each—
    Be still; they are no more.

Time, ceaseless Time, we know not when
    Thy wanderings began,
The dreamy past is sealed to us,
    The future none may scan;
We only know that round thy path
    Dark ruins have been hurled,
That 'neath thy wing Destruction rears
    His altars o'er the world.

E'en Science from his eagle height
    So little can foresee,
He silent turns abashed away
    If we but ask of thee;
And if to Eloquence we turn,
    Mute is her silver tongue,
As if upon her spirit's lyre
    The dews of death were hung.

THE PARTED YEAR.

Still onward, onward thou dost press
  With low and measured tread,
Peopling with cold and lifeless forms
  The cities of the dead;
Throwing around the young and fair
  The shadow of thy wing,
And stealing from each human heart
  Some loved and cherished thing.

Yet deep, deep in each thrilling heart
  One fount remaineth still,
Which hoary Time nor icy Death
  Hath power to touch or chill:
It is the holy fount of Love,
  Whose waters hallowed lie,
Filled from that everlasting source,
  The well-spring from on high.

We cannot stay thy footsteps, Time!
  Thy flight no hand can bind
Save His, whose foot is on the sea,
  Whose voice is in the wind;

Yet, when the stars from their bright spheres
Like living flames are hurled,
Thy mighty form will sink beneath
The ruins of the world.

I NEVER HAVE LOVED THEE.

I NEVER have loved thee; yet, strange though it be,
So soft are the feelings I cherish for thee,
That the wildest of passions could never impart
More joy to my soul, or more bliss to my heart;
They come o'er my breast in my happiest hours.
They come like the south wind, that ruffles the flowers—
A thrilling of softness, a thrilling of bliss—
Say, is there no name for a passion like this?

It cannot be friendship, it cannot be love;
Yet I know the sweet feeling descends from above;
For it takes from my bosom no portion of ease,
Yet adds all the raptures, the pleasures of these;

For so soft the emotion my spirit has nursed,
It is warm as the last, and more pure than the first;
For my heart when near thine grows as soft as a dove,
Yet it cannot be friendship, it cannot be love.

I know we must part, yet, united in soul,
Our thoughts, like one current, together will roll,
And O! should my soul be the first to ascend,
When an angel in heaven I'll plead for my friend;
Yet sometimes I think when my young life is o'er,
And my voice that hath thrilled thee, can thrill thee no more,
That my spirit will steal from its mansion of bliss
To lie on thy bosom, and guard thee in this.

Thou mayst whisper farewell, but thou canst not depart—
I hold thee too close in the folds of my heart;
And that full heart is deeper than aught else can be,
Unless 'tis the feeling I cherish for thee.
Thou canst not escape, for though wide be thy bound,
Fond memories like sentinels guard thee around—
Sweet watchers! they'll keep each intruder away,
And hold thee my captive by night and by day.

'Twere almost too sweet for such bosoms as ours
To die the calm death of the innocent flowers;
Yet, ah! if the angels will answer my prayers,
The close of our lives will be lovely as theirs—
And, O! if the death-pangs our bosoms must rend,
If they'll mingle my spirit with that of my friend,
I care not how soon they may sever earth's ties,
For, though parted on earth, we'll be linked in the skies.

LINES WRITTEN ON SEEING AN INFANT SLEEPING ON ITS MOTHER'S BOSOM.

It lay upon its mother's breast, a thing
   Bright as a dew-drop when it first descends,
Or as the plumage of an angel's wing,
   Where every tint of rainbow beauty blends;
It had soft violet eyes, that, 'neath each lid
   Half-closed upon them, like bright waters shone;
While its small dimpled hands were slily hid
   In the warm bosom that it nestled on.

There was a beam in that young mother's eye,
   Lit by the feelings that she could not speak,
As from her lips a plaintive lullaby
   Stirred the bright tresses on her infant's cheek;

While now and then, with melting heart, she pressed
    Soft kisses on its red and smiling lips,
Lips, sweet as rose-buds in fresh beauty dressed
    Ere the young murmuring bee their honey sips.

It was a fragrant eve, the sky was full
    Of burning stars, that, tremulously clear,
Shone on those lovely ones, while the low lull
    Of falling waters fell upon the ear;
And the new moon, like a pure shell of pearl
    Encircled by the blue waves of the deep,
Lay 'mid the fleecy clouds, that love to curl
    Around the stars when they their vigils keep.

My heart grew softer, as I gazed upon
    That youthful mother as she soothed to rest,
With a low song, her loved and cherished one,
    The bud of promise, on her gentle breast;
For 'tis a sight, that angel-ones above
    May stoop to gaze on from their bowers of bliss,
When Innocence upon the breast of love
    Is cradled, in a sinful world like this.

THE PRESENCE OF GOD.

O Thou, who fling'st so fair a robe
    Of clouds around the hills untrod—
Those mountain-pillars of the globe,
    Whose peaks sustain thy throne, O God!
All glittering round the sunset skies,
    Their trembling folds are lightly furled,
As if to shade from mortal eyes
    The glories of yon upper world;
There, while the evening star upholds
In one bright spot their purple folds,
My spirit lifts its silent prayer,
For Thou, the God of love, art there.

THE PRESENCE OF GOD.

The summer flowers, the fair, the sweet,
    Upspringing freely from the sod,
In whose soft looks we seem to meet,
    At every step, Thy smiles, O God!
The humblest soul their sweetness shares,
    They bloom in palace-hall, or cot—
Give me, O Lord! a heart like theirs,
    Contented with my lowly lot!
Within their pure ambrosial bells,
    In odors sweet Thy Spirit dwells;
Their breath may seem to scent the air—
    'Tis Thine, O God! for Thou art there.

List! from yon casement low and dim
    What sounds are these, that fill the breeze?
It is the peasant's evening hymn
    Arrests the fisher on the seas—
The old man leans his silver hairs
    Upon his light suspended oar,
Until those soft delicious airs
    Have died like ripples on the shore.

Why do his eyes in softness roll?
What melts the manhood from his soul?
His heart is filled with peace and prayer,
For Thou, O God! art with him there.

The birds among the summer-blooms
  Pour forth to Thee their strains of love,
When, trembling on uplifted plumes,
  They leave the earth and soar above;
We hear their sweet familiar airs
  Where'er a sunny spot is found;
How lovely is a life like theirs,
  Diffusing sweetness all around!
From clime to clime, from pole to pole,
Their sweetest anthems softly roll,
Till, melting on the realms of air,
Thy still small voice seems whispering there.

The stars, those floating isles of light,
  Round which the clouds unfurl their sails,

THE PRESENCE OF GOD.

Pure as a woman's robe of white
   That trembles round the form it veils,
They touch the heart as with a spell,
   Yet, set the soaring fancy free,
And O how sweet the tales they tell!
   They tell of peace, of love, and Thee!
Each raging storm that wildly blows,
Each balmy gale that lifts the rose,
Sublimely grand, or softly fair,
They speak of Thee, for Thou art there.

The spirit oft oppressed with doubt,
   May strive to cast Thee from its thought,
But who can shut thy presence out,
   Thou mighty Guest that com'st unsought!
In spite of all our cold resolves,
   Whate'er our thoughts, where'er we be,
Still magnet-like the heart revolves,
   And points, all trembling, up to Thee;
We cannot shield a troubled breast
Beneath the confines of the blessed,

THE PRESENCE OF GOD.

Above, below, on earth, in air,
For Thou the living God art there.

Yet, far beyond the clouds outspread,
  Where soaring fancy oft hath been,
There is a land where Thou hast said
  The pure of heart shall enter in;
In those far realms so calmly bright
  How many a loved and gentle one
Bathes its soft plumes in living light
  That sparkles from Thy radiant Throne!
There souls, once soft and sad as ours,
Look up and sing 'mid fadeless flowers—
They dream no more of grief and care,
For Thou, the God of peace, art there.

I KNOW THEE NOT.

I know thee not—I never heard thy voice,
    Yet, could I choose a friend from all mankind,
Thy spirit high should be my spirit's choice,
    Thy heart should guide my heart—thy mind, my mind!

I know not if thy features be akin
    To thy bright thoughts—or if thy lashes fall
O'er sparkling orbs—I only sigh to win
    The soul that speaks and sparkles through them all!

I know not if thou'rt blest—I hope thou art!
    Yet O! I envy her to whom belongs
The priceless treasure of thy free, high heart,
    With all its wild sweet thoughts, and sweeter songs!

I know not if thou'lt ever, ever press
    My trembling hand in thine—to meet with thee!
O! I should die for very blessedness,
    So sweetly painful would that meeting be!

I know not if thou think'st of *me* afar,
    Yet oft, I sit alone amid my flowers,
And fix my sad gaze on some still bright star,
    And muse on *thee* through long uncounted hours!

I know thou dost not—*canst not* think of me!
    Alas! my heart would leap with joy elate
Could I but hope that I might sometimes be
    A thought within thy soul—its spirit-mate!

I know not why my heart should thus be stirred
    By these wild thoughts—*thou dost not pine for me!*
And yet, how oft *I* pine to be a bird—
    A star—or any thing that's loved by thee!

I KNOW THEE NOT.

I know not if I e'er shall list thy tone,
   Or blushing, thrill beneath thy thrilling touch;
Thy songs, thy fame, are *all* my neart hath known,
   And knowing this alone—it knows too much!

THOU CANST NOT FORGET ME.

Thou canst not forget me, for memory will fling
   Her light o'er oblivion's dark sea;
And wherever thou roamest, a something will cling
   To thy bosom, that whispers of me;
Though the chords of thy spirit I now may not sweep,
   Of my touch they'll retain a soft thrill,
Like the low, under-tone of the mournful-voiced deep,
   When the wind that has swept it is still.

The love that is kept in the beauty of trust,
   Cannot pass like the foam from the seas,
Or a mark that the finger hath traced in the dust,
   When 'tis swept by the breath of the breeze;

They tell me, my love, thou wilt calmly resign,
    Yet I know, e'en while listening to them,
Thou wilt sigh for the heart that was linked unto thine
    As a rose-bud is linked to its stem.

Thou canst not forget me, too long thou hast flung
    Thy spirit's soft pinion o'er mine;
Too deep was the promise that round *my* lips clung,
    As they softly responded to *thine:*
In the hush of the twilight, beneath the blue skies
    My presence will mantle thy soul,
And a feeling of softness will rush to thine eyes,
    Too deep for thy manhood's control.

Thou mayst roam to thine own isle of beauty and fame,
    Far, far from the land of the free;
Yet, each wind that floats round thee will murmur the name
    That is softer than music to thee;
And when round thee darkly misfortunes shall crowd,
    Thou'lt think, like the beautiful form
Of the rainbow, that arches the thick tempest-cloud,
    My love would have brightened the storm.

Thou canst not forget me—the passion, that dwelt
    In the depth of thy soul, could not die,
With the memory of all thou hast murmured and felt,
    In thy bosom 'twill slumbering lie;
Thou mayst turn to another, and wish to forget,
    But the wish will not bring thee repose,
For ah! thou wilt find that the thorn of regret
    Will be linked with the sweets of the rose.

HOPELESS LOVE.

The trembling waves beneath the moonbeams quiver
    Reflecting back the blue, unclouded skies;
The stars look down upon the still bright river,
    And smile to see themselves in paradise;
Sweet songs are heard to gush in joyous bosoms,
    That lightly throb beneath the greenwood tree,
And glossy plumes float in amid the blossoms,
    And all around are happy—all but me!

And yet, I come beneath the light, that trembles
    O'er these dim paths, with listless steps to roam,
For here my bursting heart no more dissembles,
    My sad lips quiver, and the tear-drops come;

HOPELESS LOVE.

I come once more to list the low-voiced turtle,
    To watch the dreamy waters as they flow,
And lay me down beneath the fragrant myrtle,
    That drops its blossoms when the west winds blow.

O! there is one, on whose sweet face I ponder,
    One angel-being 'mid the beauteous band,
Who in the evening's hush comes out to wander
    Amid the dark-eyed daughters of the land!
Her step is lightest where each light foot presses,
    Her song is sweetest 'mid their songs of glee,
Smiles light her lips, and rose-buds, 'mid her tresses,
    Look lightly up their dark redundancy.

Youth, wealth, and fame are mine—all, that entrances
    The youthful heart, on me their charms confer;
Sweet lips smile on me too, and melting glances
    Flash up to mine—but not a glance from her!
O! I would give youth, beauty, fame, and splendor,
    My all of bliss—my every hope resign,
To wake in that young heart one feeling tender—
    To clasp that little hand, and call it mine!

HOPELESS LOVE.

In this sweet solitude the sunny weather
    Hath called to life light shapes, and fairy-elves,
The rose-buds lay their crimson lips together
    And the green leaves are whispering to themselves;
The clear, faint starlight on the blue wave flushes,
    And, filled with odors sweet, the south wind blows,
The purple clusters load the lilac-bushes,
    And fragrant blossoms fringe the apple-boughs.

Yet, I am sick with love and melancholy,
    My locks are heavy with the dropping dew,
Low murmurs haunt me—murmurs soft and holy,
    And O, my lips keep murmuring, murmuring too!
I hate the beauty of these calm, sweet bowers,
    The bird's wild music, and the fountain's fall;
O! I am sick in this lone land of flowers,
    My soul is weary—weary of them all!

Yet had I that sweet face, on which I ponder,
    To bloom for me within this Eden-home,
That lip to sweetly murmur when I wander,
    That cheek to softly dimple when I come,

How sweet would glide my days in these lone bowers,
   Far from the world and all its heartless throngs,
Her fairy feet should only tread on flowers,
   I'd make her home melodious with my songs!

Ah me! such blissful hopes once filled my bosom,
   And dreams of fame could then my heart enthrall,
And joy and bliss around me seemed to blossom,
   But O! these blissful hopes are blighted—all!
No smiling angel decks these Eden-bowers,
   No springing footstep echoes mine in glee—
O! I am weary in this land of flowers!
   I sigh—I sigh amid them all—ah me!

THE BEREAVED.

The moon within our casement beams,
   Our blue-eyed babe hath dropped to sleep,
And I have left it to its dreams,
   Amid the shadows deep,
To muse beside the silver tide,
Whose waves are rippling at thy side.

It is a still and lovely spot,
   Where they have laid thee down to rest,
The white rose and forget-me-not
   Bloom sweetly o'er thy breast,
And birds, and streams with liquid lull,
Have made the stillness beautiful.

THE BEREAVED.

And softly through the forest-bars
  Light, lovely shapes, on glossy plumes,
Float ever in, like winged stars,
  Amid the purpling glooms;
Their sweet songs, borne from tree to tree,
Thrill the light leaves with melody.

Alas! the very path I trace,
  In happier hours, thy footsteps made:
This spot was once thy resting-place,
  Within the silent shade;
Thy white hand trained the fragrant bough
That drops its blossoms o'er me now;

'Twas here at eve we used to rove,
  'Twas here I breathed my whispered vows,
And sealed them on thy lips, my love!
  Beneath the apple-boughs.
Our hearts had melted into one,
But Death undid what Love had done.

THE BEREAVED.

Alas! too deep a weight of thought
    Had filled thy heart in youth's sweet hour;
It seemed with love and bliss o'erfraught,
    A fleeting passion-flower,
Unfolding 'neath a southern sky
To blossom soon, and soon to die

Yet, in those calm and blooming bowers
    I seem to feel thy presence still,
Thy breath seems floating o'er the flowers,
    Thy whisper on the hill;
The clear, faint starlight, and the sea,
Are whispering to my heart of thee.

No more thy smiles my heart rejoice,
    Yet still I start to meet thine eye,
And call upon the low, sweet voice,
    That gives me no reply—
And list within my silent door
For the light feet that come no more.

TO LUCY DURING HER ABSENCE.

THE dew is on the blossoms, and the young moon on the sea,
It is the twilight hour—the hour for you and me—
The time when memory wanders across life's dreamy track,
When the past floats up before us, and the lost come stealing
    back;
And while along the still shore my lonely footsteps rove,
With the deep blue far beneath me, and the pale blue up above,
And with their trembling footsteps the faint stars tread the sea,
I think upon you, Lucy—do you ever think of me?

O Lucy! in this sweet hour, when the stars and waves have met,
And the full heart most remembers all it wishes to forget,
When the deep hush of the twilight seems such a holy time,
That to smile were almost sinful, and to whisper were a crime,

TO LUCY DURING HER ABSENCE.

'Tis sweet along these dim paths with lonely steps to glide,
For the moon is in the far blue, and the breeze is at my side ;
But yet my heart is heavy, and my voice hath lost its glee,
I am sighing for you, Lucy—do you ever sigh for me ?

Dear Lucy ! in your absence, where'er your wanderings tend,
You must keep within your pure heart a sweet thought for your friend,
Till you sit once more in beauty within your father's hall,
With a soft smile on your young lip, and a pleasant word for al..
Alas ! the breeze is balmy, and the hushed wave deeply blue,
And flowers are in my pathway, but no light-hearted Lu !
O the summer-months without you such a lonely time will be ?
I am sighing for you, Lucy—do you ever sigh for me ?˙

ON ENTERING THE MAMMOTH CAVE.

Hush! for my heart-blood curdles as we enter
    To glide in gloom these shadowy realms about;
Oh! what a scene the round globe to its centre,
    To form this awful cave, seems hollowed out!
Yet pause—no mystic word hath yet been spoken
    To win us entrance to this awful sphere—
A whispered prayer must be our watchword token,
And peace—like that around us—peace unbroken
        The passport here.

And now farewell, ye birds and blossoms tender,
    Ye glistening leaves by morning dews impearled,
And you, ye beams that light with softened splendor
    The glimmering glories of yon outer world!

ON ENTERING THE MAMMOTH CAVE.

While thus we pause these silent arches under,
   To you and yours a wild farewell we wave,
For oh! perhaps this awful spot may sunder
Our hearts from all we love—this world of wonder
      May be our grave.

And yet farewell! the faintly flickering torches
   Light our lone footsteps o'er the silent sod;
And now all hail, ye everlasting arches,
   Ye dark dominions of an unseen God!
Who would not for this sight the bliss surrender
   Of all the beauties of yon sunny sphere,
And break the sweetest ties, however tender,
To be the witness of the silent splendor
      That greets us here!

Ye glittering caves, ye high o'erhanging arches,
   A pilgrim-band we glide amid your gloom,
With breathless lips and high uplifted torches,
   All fancifully decked in cave-costume;

Far from the day's glad beams, and songs, and flowers,
   We've come with spell-touched hearts, ye countless caves,
To glide enchanted, for a few brief hours,
Through the calm beauty of your awful bowers
      And o'er your waves!

Beautiful cave! that all my soul entrances,
   Known as the Wonder of the West so long,
Oh 'twere a fate beyond my wildest fancies,
   Could I but shrine you now, as such in song!
But 'tis in vain—the untaught child of Nature,
   I cannot vent the thoughts that through me flow,
Yet none the less is graved thine every feature
Upon the wild imaginative creature
      That hails you now!

Palace of Nature! with a poet's fancies
   I've ofttimes pictured thee in dreams of bliss,
And glorious scenes were given to my glances,
   But never gazed I on a scene like this!

ON ENTERING THE MAMMOTH CAVE.

Compared with thine, what are the awful wonders
   Of the deep, fathomless, unbounded sea?
Or the storm-cloud whose lance of lightning sunders
The solid oak?—or even thine awful thunders,
      Niagara!

Hark! hear ye not those echoes ringing after
   Our gliding steps—my spirit faints with fear—
Those mocking tones, like subterranean laughter—
   Or does the brain grow wild with wandering here!
There may be spectres wild and forms appalling
   Our wandering eyes, where'er we rove, to greet
Methinks I hear their low sad voices calling
Upon us now, and far away the falling
      Of phantom feet.

The glittering dome, the arch, the towering column,
   Are sights that greet us now on every hand,
And all so wild—so strange—so sweetly solemn—
   So like one's fancies formed of fairy land!

ON ENTERING THE MAMMOTH CAVE.

And these then are your works, mysterious powers!
Your spells are o'er, around us, and beneath,
These opening aisles, these crystal fruits and flowers,
And glittering grots and high-arched beauteous bowers,
    As still as death!

But yet lead on! perhaps than this fair vision,
    Some lovelier yet in darkling distance lies—
Some cave of beauty, like those realms elysian
    That ofttimes open on poetic eyes!
Some spot, where led by fancy's sweet assistance
    Our wandering feet o'er silvery sands may stray,
Where prattling waters urge with soft resistance
Their wavelets on, till lost in airy distance,
    And far away!

Oft the lone Indian o'er these low-toned waters
    Has bent perhaps his swarthy brow to lave!
It seems the requiem of their dark-eyed daughters—
    Those sweet wild notes that wander o'er the wave!

ON ENTERING THE MAMMOTH CAVE.

Hast thou no relic of their ancient glory,
   No legend, lonely cavern! linked with thine?
No tale of love—no wild romantic story
Of some warm heart whose dreams were transitory
      And sweet as mine?

It must be so! the thought your spell enhances—
   Yet why pursue this wild, romantic dream?
The heart, afloat upon its fluttering fancies,
   Would lose itself in the bewildering theme!
And yet, ye waters! still I list your surging,
   And ever and anon I seem to view,
In fancy's eye, some Indian maid emerging
Through the deep gloom, and o'er your waters urging
      Her light canoe.

Oh silent cave! amid the elevation
   Of lofty thought could I abide with thee,
My soul's sad shrine, my heart's lone habitation,
   Forever and forever thou shouldst be!

Here into song my every thought I'd render,
  And thou—and thou alone—shouldst be my theme,
Far from the weary world's delusive splendor,
Would not my lonely life be all one tender
  Delicious dream?

Yes! though no other form save mine might hover
  In these lone halls, no other whisper roll
Along those airy domes that arch me over
  Save gentle Echo's, sister of my soul!
Yet, 'neath these domes whose spell of beauty weighs me,
  My heart would evermore in bliss abide—
No sorrow to depress, no hope to raise me,
Here would I ever dwell—with none to praise me
  And none to chide!

Region of caves and streams! and must I sever
  My spirit from your spell? 'Twere bliss to stray
The happy rover of your realms forever,
  And yet, farewell forever and for aye!

I leave you now, yet many a sparkling token
　Within your cool recesses I have sought
To treasure up with fancies still unspoken—
Till from these quivering heart-strings, Death hath broken
　The thread of thought!

SUDDEN DEATH.

How still she lies upon her pillow sinking,
   With her white folded hands upon her breast !
The rosy morn disturbs not her sweet thinking—
   And fails the lark to rouse her from her rest.
She sleeps as if her soul exhaled in sighs—
As if her lover's kisses closed her eyes !

How still she lies ! But list—through her hushed chamber
   A sudden sound of childish glee hath spread ;
While little forms with laughing voices clamber
   O'er ner soft bosom, and about her bed.
They toss their golden locks before her eyes,
Crying in sportive tones—" Rise, sister, rise !

"Oh, rise! We've been away among the flowers,
    And had such gambols with the bird and bee!
The young things thought to give us chase for hours,
    But were not lighter on the wing than we.
And see! we stole their buds and flowers in play—
Oh, rise, sweet sister—rise and come away!"

Alas, ye glad young creatures! o'er that fair
    And polished cheek your kisses fall in vain.
No sister's voice can wake the stillness there,
    Nor bring the red-rose to that cheek again!
Nor wake those smiles—nor bow that lovely head
To meet your soft embraces—she is dead!

Away! bear back your buds and blossoms fair—
    Break not the stillness of that awful room!
Your cheerful tones awake no echo there—
    Would that your glee could gladden up its gloom.
But 'tis in vain—Death shadows o'er the spot—
Bear back your buds and flowers—she heeds them not!

SUDDEN DEATH.

But for the spell that now her fair form cumbers,
   Soon had she flown your fairy forms to meet;
But Death o'ertook her in her rosy slumbers,
   And hushed her answering voice—and chained her feet!
And now with moveless lips and closed eyes,
Pale on her couch your darling sister lies.

Alas! that lovely sister! Yesternight
   She moved the fairest 'mid the festive throng,
With step so joyous, and with voice so light,
   That Music's self seemed discord to its song.
Fair, and exulting in youth's fleeting breath,
How long to her seemed life—how distant death!

And when upon her pillow soft and still,
   With her blue eye fixed on the moon's pale beams,
Guileless of heart, and thinking of no ill,
   And gliding off, so sweetly, to her dreams—
Death's awful shadow o'er her slumber passed!
But life to her was lovely to the last.

Translated thus to lovelier worlds than ours,
   Without a pang, she knows not of decay,
Nor how she wandered to those blissful bowers,
   Nor what it was that stole her breath away.
Nor feels her bark, safe moored in Heaven at last—
To reach that Heaven—the dreary gulf it passed!

Brief was her sojourn in youth's beauteous bowers—
   She floated calm adown life's glittering tide,
Bright as the beams, and fragrant as the flowers
   Amid whose glowing hues she lived and died—
Ere fickle friendship filled her heart with tears,
Or passion marred the peace of her young years.

And she is dead! Death's cold and withering touch
   Hath quenched in that young breast life's perfumed flame.
She whom her fair young sisters loved so much!
   She whom her parents dear delight to name!
Frail is the tenure of our mortal breath—
Yea, "in the midst of life we are in death!"

I SAW THEE BUT A MOMENT.

I saw thee but a moment—thou sad and lovely one !
I saw thee but a moment—yet my heart was *then* undone !
Thou didst dawn upon my spirit, in all thy bloom and truth,
A passing vision given to my warm and yearning youth.

I saw thee but a moment—'twas 'mid the festive throng.
Some happy youths were round thee—they had pleaded for a song—
The last guests were departing—and I, too, had said "good night,"
When thy gush of song o'ertook me—and chained me with delight !

I SAW THEE BUT A MOMENT.

I turned—and oh that vision!—thy beauty, fair unknown!
Still thrills me with a power that I almost dread to own—
There were brighter ones around thee in that gay and brilliant hall,
But the sweetest face among them, was the saddest face of all!

I know not what came o'er me in the tumult of that hour—
There were burning thoughts within me—of passion and of power!
How sweetly throbbed my bosom, as I listened to thy lay,
But my peace of heart was over, ere the last note died away!

I know not what came o'er me 'mid that hushed and listening band,
As I strove to nerve the spirit that thy music had unmanned.
I heard some murmured praises—and thy low and sweet replies—
While harp—and throng—and singer—all swam before my eyes!

The siren-song was ended—and I paused to ask thy name—
At the memory of that moment, even now, I blush for shame;
But the wild blood of my boyhood throbbed at my bosom's core—
I heard that thou wert wedded—and fainted on the floor!

The time is past and over—and my dreams have changed since
    then—
I have learned to mask my spirit, in my intercourse with men!
But the feelings of that moment—unconscious of control—
Still send their glowing current like lava through my soul!

The time is past and over—and though madness it may be—
There are moments still, lost beauty! when I pause to think of
    thee!
When I seem to feel thy glances—as they thrilled my heart of
    yore—
But the memory hath unmanned me—I must think of thee no
    more!

THE EVENING SKIES.

Soft skies! amid your halls to-night
   How brightly beams each starry sphere!
Beneath your softly mellowed light
   The loveliest scenes grow lovelier!
How high, how great, the glorious Power
   That bade these silvery dew-drops fall;
That touched with bloom the folded flower,
   And bent the blue sky over all.

I love to glide in these still hours
   With heart, and thought, and fancy free,
When naught but stars, and waves, and flowers,
   May give me their sweet company!

THE EVENING SKIES. 253

When far below the waves outspread
  Glide softly on with liquid hue;
When winds are low—and skies o'erhead
  Are beaming beautifully blue.

Oh, what a heavenly hour is this!
  The green earth seems an Eden-home,—
And yet I pine amid my bliss,
  For purer blisses yet to come!
How can my spirit gaze aloft
  Upon your deep delicious blue,
And float to those far realms so oft,
  And never sigh to flutter through?

And yet this spot, so still, so lone,
  Seems formed to suit my mournful mood,
The far blue heavens seem all my own,
  And all this lovely solitude!
A voice seems whispering on the hill
  Soft as my own—and on the sea
A living spirit seems to thrill
  And throb with mine deliciously!

Yet, though my thoughts from care seem freed,
    And a soft joy pervades my breast,
That makes me almost feel indeed
    That hearts on earth are sometimes blessed!
There is a spell in those hushed skies—
    A something felt in this lone spot,
That makes my very soul arise
    With longings for—it knows not what!

Beneath such skies I sometimes doubt
    My heart can e'er have dreamed of sin—
The world seems all so calm without,
    And all my thoughts so pure within!
Such dreams play o'er my folded lid!
    Such heavenly visions greet my view!
I almost seem to glide amid
    The angel-bands, an angel too!

THE OLD MAID.

Why sits she thus in solitude? her heart
    Seems melting in her eye's delicious blue,—
And as it heaves, her ripe lips lie apart
    As if to let its heavy throbbings through;
In her dark eye a depth of softness swells,
    Deeper than that her careless girlhood wore;
And her cheek crimsons with the hue that tells
    The rich, fair fruit is ripened to the core.

It is her thirtieth birthday! with a sigh
    Her soul hath turned from youth's luxuriant bowers,
And her heart taken up the last sweet tie .
    That measured out its links of golden hours!

She feels her inmost soul within her stir
  With thoughts too wild and passionate to speak;
Yet her full heart—its own interpreter—
  Translates itself in silence on her cheek

Joy's opening buds, affection's glowing flowers,
  Once lightly sprang within her beaming track;
Oh, life was beautiful in those lost hours!
  And yet she does not wish to wander back!
No! she but loves in loneliness to think
  On pleasures past, though never more to be:
Hope links her to the future—but the link
  That binds her to the past is memory!

From her lone path she never turns aside,
  Though passionate worshippers before her fall;
Like some pure planet in her lonely pride,
  She seems to soar and beam above them all!
Not that her heart is cold! emotions new
  And fresh as flowers, are with her heart-strings knit.
And sweetly mournful pleasures wander through
  Her virgin soul, and softly ruffle it.

THE OLD MAID.

For she hath lived with heart and soul alive
 To all that makes life beautiful and fair;
Sweet thoughts, like honey-bees, have made their hive
 Of her soft bosom-cell, and cluster there;
Yet life is not to her what it hath been,—
 Her soul hath learned to look beyond its gloss—
And now she hovers like a star between
 Her deeds of love—her Saviour on the Cross!

Beneath the cares of earth she does not bow,
 Though she hath ofttimes drained its bitter cup,
But ever wanders on with heavenward brow,
 And eyes whose lovely lids are lifted up!
She feels that in that lovelier, happier sphere,
 Her bosom yet will, bird-like, find its mate,
And all the joys it found so blissful here
 Within that spirit-realm perpetuate.

Yet, sometimes o'er her trembling heart-strings thrill
 Soft sighs, for raptures it hath ne'er enjoyed,—
And then she dreams of love, and strives to fill
 With wild and passionate thoughts the craving void.

And thus she wanders on—half sad, half blest—
Without a mate for the pure, lonely heart,
That, yearning, throbs within her virgin breast,
Never to find its lovely counterpart!

THE BROTHER'S LAMENT.

ONE moment more, beneath the old elm, Mary,
    Where last we parted in the flowing dell—
One moment more through twilight tints that vary,
    To gaze upon thy grave, and then, farewell!
Ere from this spot, and these loved scenes I sever,
    Where still thy lovely spirit seems to stray—
One look—to fix them on my soul forever—
    And then away!

Mary, I know my steps should now be shrinking
    From this sad spot—but on my mournful gaze
A scene floats up that sets my soul to thinking
    On all the dear delights of other days!
I'm gazing on the little foot-bridge yonder,
    Thrown o'er the stream whose waters purl below,
Where I so oft have seen thee pause and ponder,
    Leaning thy white brow on thy hand of snow.

THE BROTHER'S LAMENT.

I'm standing on the spot where last we parted,
    Where, as I left thee in the fragrant dell,
I saw thee turn so oft—half broken-hearted—
    Waving thy hand in token of farewell.
I start to meet thy footstep light and airy—
    But—the cold grass waves o'er thy sweet young head;
Would that the shroud that wraps thy fair form, Mary,
    Wrapped mine instead!

In vain my heart its bitter thoughts would parry,
    An adder's grasp about its chords seems curled,
For you were all I ever thought of, Mary—
    Were all I doted on in this wide world!
And yet, I'd sigh not while thy fate I ponder,
    Did memory only bring thee to my eyes
Pale as thou sleepest in the churchyard yonder—
    Or as an angel dazzling from the skies!
I then at least could treasure each sweet token
    Of thy pure love—and in life's mad'ning whirl
Steel my crushed heart—had not thine own been broken,
    Poor hapless girl!

But, Mary—Mary, when I think upon thee,
    As when I last beheld thee in thy pride—
And on the fate—O God!—to which *he* won thee—
    I curse the hour that sent me from your side!
O why wert thou so richly, strangely gifted
    With mortal loveliness beyond compare?
The look of love beneath thy lashes lifted—
    Its fatal sweetness was to thee a snare!
Yet sleep, my sister—I will not upbraid thee—
    Thou wert too sweet—too innocently dear;
But he—the exulting demon who betrayed thee—
    He lives, he lives, and I am loitering here!
Even now some happier fair one's chains may bind him
    In dalliance sweet—but I'll avenge thee well!
Avenge thee?—Yes! a brother's curse will find him,
    Though he should dive into the deeps of hell!
I swear it, sister—as thou art forgiven—
    By all our wrongs—by all our severed ties,
And by the blessedness of yon blue heaven,
    That gives its world of azure to mine eyes!
By all my love—by every sacred duty
    A brother owes—and by yon heaving sod,

THE BROTHER'S LAMENT.

Thine early grave—and by thy blighted beauty,
   Thou sweetest angel in the realms of God!
I swear it, by the bursting groans I smother,
   And call on Heaven and thee to nerve me now.
Mary, look down!—behold thy wretched brother,
     And bless the vow!

Sister, my soul its last farewell is taking,
   And I for this had thought it nerved to-night,
But every chord about my heart seems breaking,
   And blinding tears shut out the glimmering sight.
One look—one last long look to hill and meadow—
   To the old foot-bridge and the murmuring mill,
And to the churchyard sleeping in the shadow—
   Cease tears—and let these fond eyes look their fill!
One look—and now farewell ye scenes that vary
   Beneath the twilight shades that round me flow!
The charm that bound my wild heart here, was Mary—
     And she lies low!

ONE WORD WITH THEE.

ONE word with thee—one sweet yet mournful meeting,
　If but to catch again thy low sad tone,
And clasp thy hand, and feel its warm pulse beating
　With love's delicious throb against my own!
If but to catch thine eye, and hear thee say—
"I will remember thee when far away."

One word with thee—though not of hope or gladness,
　On which to muse when we are far apart;
A whisper—breathed in silence and in sadness—
　To leave a hush forever on my heart!
One word—to treasure in my bosom-core,
Whether we meet again, or meet no more.

ONE WORD WITH THEE.

One word with thee—though it may be to sever
  The last sweet link that binds thy soul to mine,
And tear me from thy burning heart forever,
  To place another on its shattered shrine!
One word—to treasure in my bosom-core,
Whether we meet again, or meet no more.

One word with thee—one brief yet blissful meeting
  To catch thy voice, where last we met alone;
Whose faintest sigh can set this heart to beating
  With thoughts and feelings that it dare not own!
One word—O God of bliss, and can it be
That it may be our last?—One word with thee!

THE END.

www.ingramcontent.com/pod-product-compliance
Lightning Source LLC
Chambersburg PA
CBHW032149230426
43672CB00011B/2499